# OTSEGO COUNTY
## NEW YORK

### GEOGRAPHICAL
### AND HISTORICAL

From the Earliest Settlement
to the Present Time

— WITH —

COUNTY AND TOWNSHIP MAPS
FROM ORIGINAL DRAWINGS

— BY —

*Edwin F. Bacon, Ph.B.*

Previously Published as Pipe Creek Publicatons'
*Early Settler Series: New York, No. 5*

HERITAGE BOOKS
2011

# HERITAGE BOOKS

*AN IMPRINT OF HERITAGE BOOKS, INC.*


## Books, CDs, and more—Worldwide

For our listing of thousands of titles see our website
at
www.HeritageBooks.com


Published 2011 by
HERITAGE BOOKS, INC.
Publishing Division
100 Railroad Ave. #104
Westminster, Maryland 21157

Originally published: Oneonta, New York
The Oneonta Herald, Publishers
1902

Published 1993 by Pipe Creek Publications
Finksburg, Maryland
(not a facsimile reprint)

*Pipe Creek's Early Settler Series
New York, No. 5*

International Standard Book Numbers
Paperbound: 978-1-58549-840-6
Clothbound: 978-0-7884-8875-7

## PREFACE

There is a growing demand for the means of local geographical and historical study in schools, and this little manual is intended to meet this demand for the schools of Otsego County. It was originally prepared in manuscript for classes in the Oneonta State Normal school and now, with the approval and encouragement of the school commissioners and teachers of the county, is offered in its present form.

In its preparation I have had the pleasure of visiting every township in the county, thus gaining information at first hand and from the most reliable sources. For events previous to our time, I have found excellent material. The history of the county from the earliest times to 1878, by D. Hamilton Hurd, is very complete to that date, and I have, with permission, freely quoted from it. In addition to this I have had access to Campbell's "Annals of Tyron County," Beardsley's "Reminiscences and Anecdotes," and Halsey's "Old New York Frontier,"--three works of surpassing interest, together with a number of local sketches, including Sawyer's "History of Cherry Valley," Ward's "Annals of Richfield," Campbell's "History of Oneonta," Shaw's "History of Cooperstown," Halsey's "Pioneers of Unadilla," and Hotchkin's "History of Maryland." I am also indebted to the supervisors of the several townships and to others for careful revision of the township maps and of the text, by which the greatest accuracy has been secured.

While making this study, an opinion previously formed has been essentially modified. That opinion was that farming in Otsego county had, owing to western competition and other causes, ceased to be profitable; that there were many abandoned farms, and that the rising generation thought only of getting away from the old homestead and seeking employment elsewhere. All such views must be due to the depression of former years, for they are no longer true to the facts. The increase in rural prosperity evident throughout the state is equally apparent in this region. Owing to the tendency of population toward the villages there are some abandoned farmhouses, but there are no abandoned farm lands in the county, and the intelligent and thrifty farmer is everywhere doing well. This improvement is most evident in the line of dairying, which is now the leading and most profitable industry.

Otsego county has a most interesting and honorable record. Its early settlers were of good New England and old England stock, and their numerous descendants here and in the west, to which many of them have gone, must read with interest the record of pioneer struggles, of victory over savage and foreign foes, of heroic strife for the Union, of modern culture and enterprise.

The study of geography properly commences around the home. The perspective of world study is better from this standpoint, and the children who become thoroughly interested in it will go on to the study of their own and foreign countries with a clearer idea of its nature and importance. The prevailing interest in local geography is therefore to be encouraged by every means, and it is hoped that this little contribution to it may prove acceptable to the teachers of the county.

---

While primarily intended as a school text book, the requirements of the business world have also been kept in view in the preparation of this work. The county and township maps, all from original drawings, are thoroughly up to date, and the descriptive text concerning routes of travel, population, post-offices, newspapers, business and manufacturing interests, express, telegraph and telephone facilities, commend it to all classes, while its business-like quality can in no wise impair its usefulness in the class-room.

E.F.B.

Oneonta, New York, August, 1902.

MAP of OTSEGO COUNTY NEW YORK to accompany Bacon's History

# OTSEGO COUNTY

-------

## PART I--GENERAL HISTORY

-------

Location And Political Origin.

TSEGO COUNTY is favorably situated upon the highlands at the head waters of the Susquehanna river, a
little southeast of the center of the state, and contains
1,038 square miles. It is bounded by the following named
counties: On the north by Oneida, Herkimer and Montgomery; on the east by Schoharie; on the south by Delaware; and
on the west by Chenango and Madison.

It was originally a part of Albany county, which was
organized in 1683, and which covered a large section of the
state, and the whole of the present state of Vermont. In the
year 1772 Tryon county was set off from Albany county. In
1784 the name Tryon was changed to Montgomery and in
1791 Otsego was set off from Montgomery with Cooperstown
as its county seat. As thus formed the county, although with
its present dimensions, was divided into only two townships,
viz." Otsego lying to the west of Otsego Lake and the Susquehanna, and Cherry Valley to the east of those waters. With
the increase of population these townships were again and
again subdivided until the number is now twenty-four, as
shown in the accompanying map.

### NATURAL FEATURES.

The surface presents a great variety of hill and dale
with many beautiful landscapes. In every township are found
elevations of from 250 to 500 feet, among which flow a great
number of small streams. The greatest elevations are in
Cherry Valley township, where several hills rise more than
2,000 feet above tide. The most important water courses are

1

the Unadilla river, which constitutes the western boundary, the Susquehanna flowing down centrally from Otsego Lake and constituting a portion of the southern boundary, Wharton and Butternuts creeks, flowing into the Unadilla river; Otego, Schenevus and Cherry Valley creeks, flowing into the Susquehanna, and Oaks creek, the outlet of Canadarago Lake, flowing also into the Susquehanna. Otsego Lake, the largest body of water in this region, lies within the townships of Otsego, Springfield and Middlefield. It is eight miles long and about one mile wide. It lies about 1,200 feet above sea level, and is surrounded by hills that rise from 400 to 500 feet above its surface. It is a lake of unsurpassed beauty, and many excursions are made upon it by means of steamers and other pleasure boats. Its banks are also dotted with summer camps and cottages. This lake has been made famous as the scene of Cooper's novels, "The Deerslayer," and "The Pioneer."

## THE SIX NATIONS

This region, before the advent of the white man, has been described as an "Indian Paradise." It was a superb hunting ground, the home of the deer, the elk, the moose, the bear, the otter, the martin, the wolf, the fox, the squirrel, and of numerous water fowl, while salmon and other fish abounded in the rivers and lakes.

The natives belonged to a famous Indian league called by the English the "Six Nations," though the French applied to them the general term "Iroquois."

It is well to know something of the origin and history of this league, for the colonial settlers throughout the state had much to do with it. It is supposed to have been formed about the year 1600, and consisted at first of five tribes--the Onondagas, Oneidas, Mohawks, Cayugas, and Senecas. Later it received the Tuscaroras, who came from North Carolina. It was with the Mohawks and Tuscaroras that the white settlers had most to do. These Indians were fierce and aggressive. From this far east to the Mississippi they were known and dreaded by other tribes, none of whom were able to resist them. "I have been told," says Colden, "by old men in New England who remember the time when the Mohawks made war upon the Indians, that, as soon as a single Mohawk

2

was discovered in their country, the Indians raised the cry from hill to hill, 'A Mohawk! a Mohawk!' upon which they fled like sheep before wolves without attempting to make the least resistance."

The first whites who came in contact with the tribes of this confederacy were the French, who lived in peace with them, and the Indians sided with them against the English in the "Old French war" (1754-1763). Later, when the English had triumphed over the French, they made friendly treaties with these Indians and thus received their assistance against the rebellious colonists. And so it happened that in the war of the Revolution the English, the Tories and the Indians were combined against the patriots who were fighting for independence. The scattered settlements were almost defenceless against this strong combination of enemies, and all the more so because very many of the best men were enlisted in the colonial army and thus were far from the homes that so much needed them for defence. All the horrors of that period resulted from this condition of things, but the Indians, from their standpoint, had a good excuse for making war upon the patriot settlers, for previous to the war they had made a treaty offensive and defensive with the English, and as allies were bound to join them in their war upon the "rebels."

But at the close of the Revolution the poor Indians paid a terrible penalty for being on the wrong side in that struggle. At first the feeling against them was so strong that they came near being destroyed or driven out of the state, but through the influence of Washington and others they were assigned to reservations, and measures were taken for their civilization and education. The few Indians now remaining in the state are the descendants of those fierce warriors of the olden time.

### THE FIRST WHITE SETTLEMENTS.

According to Halsey, "white men appear to have been in the upper Susquehanna valley in 1616, or about one hundred and sixty years before the revolution. They came as explorers and then as traders. After them in the next century came missionaries to the Indians. Finally, in 1769, arrived surveyors." ("The Pioneers of Unadilla Village," by Francis W. Halsey.)

3

The first grant of land to white settlers in this region was made in the year 1738, and consisted of about 8,000 acres, located in the northeast part of the present county of Otsego. It was granted by George Clark, the lieutenant governor of New York, to four men--John Lindesay, Jacob Roseboom, Lenelet Ganesvoort, and Sybrant VanSchaick. The originator and leader of this settlement, Mr. Lindesay, was a Scotchman, a man of wealth and culture. The others, judging from their names, must have been of the old Dutch stock. Their settlement was at Cherry Valley.

These pioneers, with their families, suffered many privations during the first years of their settlement, and in the winter of 1740-41, would have perished but for the assistance of a friendly Mohawk who came to them from the Mohawk valley on snow shoes and, learning their destitute condition, made repeated trips to his home, bringing back provisions. This kindness was the result of Mr. Lindesay's generous treatment of the Indians from the beginning. He had made them his fast friends and received in turn the same kindness that William Penn and all other settlers experienced who were just and friendly to these trusting children of nature.

In 1741 the little settlement was increased by the arrival of five families originally from the north of Ireland. The heads of these families were Rev. Samuel Dunlop, David Ramsay, William Gallt, James Campbell and William Dickson. They added about thirty persons to the community. During the next ten years only four new families came. Mr. Lindesay had retired from the settlement, having gone into the military service, and trouble had broken out with the Indians so that progress was retarded by constant fear of an Indian war. In 1762 there were only eight families, and during the French and Indian war it became necessary to build a fort at Cherry Valley, at which a company of soldiers was stationed. But no serious hostilities took place, and at the beginning of the Revolution the settlement numbered three hundred persons.

The town of Edmeston was settled about 1770 by Col. Edmeston, a former officer of the English army, who received a tract of 10,000 acres for his services in the French war.

Hartwick dates from a grant made to John Christopher Hartwick, in the year 1761.

In Laurens the first settlement was made by Joseph Mayall in 1774.

Middlefield was settled in 1755 by William Cook and others. In 1773 Ebenezer Knapp from Dutchess county settled on Butternuts creek in the town of Morris.

Increase Thurston and Benjamin Lull settled in New Lisbon in 1773.

Henry Schramling and families bearing the name of Young and Alger settled in Oneonta township before the Revolution, but the exact date is not known.

There were several other small settlements within the present limits of the county before the Revolution, as at Milford, Exeter, Unadilla, and Richfield Springs; but they assumed no importance until after the war.

## OTSEGO COUNTY DURING THE REVOLUTION.

Up to the time of the Revolution the settlers in this region had managed to keep on tolerably good terms with the Indians, but with the outbreak of the war of independence a great change occurred. It was a question which side the Indians would take in the impending conflict. They would perhaps have sided with the colonists or remained neutral had it not been for the opposing influence of one man, Sir William Johnson, who had long been among them as the agent of the British government, and who had dealt very justly with them. This man found means of uniting five of the "Six Nations" against the patriot settlers. The Oneidas, although friendly to the British, refused to fight against the colonies and consequently their territory was ravaged by the tories. Throughout the struggle the Indians, encouraged by the English loyalists and tories, carried on a merciless warfare against the scattered and feeble settlements of central New York and Pennsylvania.

In July, 1778, occurred the great massacre of Wyoming, a village on the Susquehanna river in Pennsylvania, and in the following November a like fate befell the settlement at Cherry Valley. This latter disaster might have been averted if the warnings given had been promptly heeded by the officer in command of the small garrison stationed at that place, for a fort had been built and all the inhabitants might have been brought within it. But the commander, Col. Alden, seemed to doubt the truth of the warnings although they came in an official communication from the officer in command at Fort Schuyler. He was one of the first to be killed as he retreated, bravely, defending himself, toward the fort. In this massacre thirty-two of the settlers together with sixteen soldiers acting as a guard outside of the fort were slain. The fort itself, being defended with cannon, held out against the several assaults made upon it. Failing in these attacks, the savages set fire to all the dwellings outside the fortifications, and retreated down the Cherry Valley creek taking with them as prisoners about seventy of the inhabitants, though nearly all of these were soon released and permitted to return in safety. The military post was maintained until the next summer, when it was abandoned. A second attack and massacre in 1780 compelled the remaining inhabitants to flee for safety, and the place was thus entirely deserted until after the close of the war.

These and other Indian massacres aroused the general government to an act of terrible retribution. A campaign of destruction was organized under the command of Generals Sullivan and Clinton, who received orders to attack and destroy without mercy all the villages of the hostile tribes of the state. General Sullivan, who was chief in command, first marched from his camp on the Hudson (May 1st, 1779), to the scene of the late massacre in the Wyoming valley. From thence he moved to Tioga Point at the confluence of the Chemuing and Susquehanna rivers and built a fort which he called Fort Sullivan. In the meantime Gen. Clinton with 1800 men ascended the Mohawk river, from the Hudson to Canajoharie. He thence made the portage to Otsego Lake with the intention of descending the Susquehanna river to Tioga Point, there to form a junction with Gen. Sullivan. He had transported a large number of boats across the country from the Mohawk for this purpose. In these he descended the lake, but found the river too low to float them, upon which he devised a very ingenious means of raising the water. He dammed up the outlet of the lake until the water rose nearly three feet, then having all in readiness, and his boats distributed along the banks, he cut the dam and so safely floated down on the swelling current.

The Indians along the course of the river were greatly astonished at this phenomenon. First the water fell, and then suddenly and without any visible cause, rose, bearing upon its bosom a hostile fleet. They regarded this as an interposition of the Great Spirit in favor of their enemies, and so fled in terror from their villages, leaving the invaders to make their journey unmolested. Only a portion of the force kept to the boats, the greater part marching along the banks of the river. The junction with Sullivan was safely made and the combined forces, now numbering 3,200 men, advanced northward on a mission of devastation through the rich Indian settlements, of the Chemung and Genesee valleys. All the villages were burned, the numerous fine orchards cut down, and immense quantities of corn destroyed. The Indians, after making a brave stand and being defeated at Newtown, on the present site of Elmira, fled to the protection of the British forts at Niagara, around which they encamped and where they spent the winter in great distress, but their spirit was not broken and they were soon again upon the warpath, continuing their depredations upon the white settlements until the close of the Revolution.

But the field of conflict was changed from the Susquehanna to the Mohawk and Schoharie, for on the upper Susquehanna there remained nothing to fight for and no one to fight. Successive conquests by both parties had given the whole region back to nature and to the wild beasts. Almost the only human beings who now traversed it were those who followed the ancient trails on their way to the new battle grounds beyond.

It was thus that Otsego county, which had nearly a dozen white settlements at the beginning of the Revolution, was an uninhabited wilderness at its close, but with peace a new era was soon to dawn upon it.

## THE FORMATION OF TOWNSHIPS.

Gen. Sullivan's devastating march made Central New York better known to the whites than ever before, and as soon as released from military service many of his officers and men hastened to return as peaceful settlers to a region through

7

which they had so recently passed as destroyers. A great tide of emigration also set in from the New England states.

The settlements made before the war and abandoned during the Indian troubles were also quickly revived as soon as peace returned, and from that time the population rapidly increased, as is apparent from the formation of new townships immediately following the organization of the county in 1791. Between that date and the end of the century, nine years, eleven new townships were formed by subdividing the original ones, viz.: Burlington, Butternuts, Exeter, Middlefield, Milford, Pittsfield, Plainfield, Richfield, Springfield, Unadilla and Worcester. Between 1800 and 1810 seven more townships were formed, viz.: Decatur, Edmeston, Hartwick, Laurens, Maryland, New Lisbon, and Westford. Otego was formed in 1822, and Oneonta in 1830. Morris was taken from Butternuts in 1849, and Roseboom from Cherry Valley in 1854.

## POPULATION.

The population of Otsego county increased with wonderful rapidity from its organization in 1791 up to about 1830, since which time it has remained nearly stationary, although some of the villages have gained. In 1790 the population of the county was 1,702, in 1800 it was 21,634, in 1810 it was 38,802, in 1820 it was 44,856, and in 1830 it was 51,372. The largest population recorded at any census was in 1880, when it was 51,397, or twenty-five more than in 1830. Since then the villages have gained about six thousand, while the rural population has had more than this number. In 1890 the population was 50,801, and in 1900 it was 48,939.

## OTSEGO COUNTY IN THE REBELLION.

Otsego contributed its full quota of men to the union cause. The total number of enlistments credited to the county was 2,925, distributed among 129 regiments in all departments of the service--infantry, cavalry and artillery. The largest proportion of Otsego men were found in the 51st, 76th, 121st, and 152d regiments of state infantry, in the 3d

8

cavalry, in the 1st, 2d and 3d artillery, and in the 1st engineer corps. 87 enlisted in the U.S. regular army and 146 in the navy. In addition to these 526 are recorded as enlisting without mention of the regiment or branch of the service to which they were assigned.

The bombardment and capture of Fort Sumter in Charleston harbor in April, 1861, was the real beginning of the war. It was immediately followed by the President's call for 75,000 volunteers to defend the government and suppress the rebellion. To this call Otsego made a prompt response. A company was organized at Cherry Valley of which George W. Tuckerman was captain and Egbert Olcott and Cleveland J. Campbell lieutenants. It was however not quite soon enough to be accepted for that service. Those were days of prompt enlistment, and the required number had been received before the Cherry Valley company reported at Albany. Its members joined other companies a little later.

The next organized movement in the county was also at Cherry Valley, where the 39th regiment of New York State National Guards had for many years been quartered. In September, 1861, this regiment authorized its Colonel, John D. Shaul, to offer its services for the war. The next month Gen. George E. Danforth, the commander of the brigade to which the 39th belonged, came to Cherry Valley and established a military post. The 39th was then recruited and organized for the war to the number of six companies with a total of 500 men. In this incomplete form it was ordered to Albany, and its several companies assigned to other regiments, there being no time to wait for it to fill up its ranks and go as a unit. Two companies, those of Captains E. N. Hanson and N. Bowdish, were transferred to the 3d New York artillery, and those of Captains A. L. Swan, J. E. Cook and J. W. Young to the 76th infantry. The following are brief sketches of some of the regiments that contained Otsego county men:

The Fifty-First.--Company I of this regiment was recruited principally in Otsego county. It saw hard and heroic service both in the east and west. At Antietam the regiment lost ninety-five men in five minutes. At Fredericksburg, in Sumner's corps, it lost six color bearers and eighty men. Its flag was the first to wave over Jackson, Miss. Of

1,200 men who went out in this regiment, only 200 returned at the close of the war.

The Seventy-Sixth.--The majority of the men of this regiment were from Courtland county, but three companies were from Otsego. Its first commander was Nelson W. Green of Courtland, and the second William P. Wainright, under whose strict discipline it became famous. It served three years and took part in nearly all the great battles in Virginia, especially distinguishing itself and suffering heavy losses at Gainesville, South Mountain and the second Bull Run. At Gettysburg it formed part of the first army corps under General Reynolds, and it was in that terrible struggle on Willoughby Run, where on the first day the fate of the army depended upon holding the position while other divisions moved to take possession of Cemetery Ridge. The 76th went into this action with 348 men and 27 officers, and in half an hour it lost two officers killed and sixteen wounded, 30 men killed and 116 wounded. It was here that General Reynolds was killed. This corps was splendidly commanded by three men who in succession fell in battle while leading it, viz.: Reynolds, at Gettysburg; Wadsworth, in the Wilderness, and Rice at Spottsylvania, all within a single year, and the last named after being in command but two days. On the expiration of three years for which the 76th enlisted, 165 of its members re-enlisted and were transferred to the 147th, an Oswego regiment, with whom they served until the close of the war.

The One Hundred and Twenty-First was recruited in Otsego and Herkimer counties. Its first colonel was Hon. Richard Franchot of Morris, and its first Major was Egbert Olcott of Cherry Valley. Its second Colonel was Emory Upton, one of the ablest and bravest officers in the service, a graduate of West Point, and under him the regiment became famous. The records of the war department credit this regiment with taking part in 25 battles, including Fredericksburg, Gettysburg, The Wilderness, Spottsylvania, Petersburg and the final series of engagements that ended with the surrender of Lee and the close of the war. It had 14 officers and 212 men killed in battle, 27 officers and 596 men wounded. On the Gettysburg battlefield as been erected a monument commemorative of the part taken by the 121st in that battle. It is of Quincy granite and bronze, and is surmounted by the figure of a soldier. It bears, besides the historical inscription, a bronze medallion of General Emory Upton, life size. This regiment contained 483 Otsego county men.

The One Hundred and Fifty-Second: This regiment, like the 121st, was raised in the twentieth senatorial district, which comprised the counties of Otsego and Herkimer. It was recruited at Camp Schuyler across the Mohawk from the village of Herkimer and was mustered into the United States service at that place October 15, 1862. It was immediately sent to Virginia, where it was actively engaged until the close of the war, except during the summer of 1863, when it was sent to New York city to aid in the suppression of the draft riots. Its hardest service occurred after General Grant took command of the Army of the Potomac. It was then engaged in the battle of the Wilderness, at Cold Harbor, and at the siege of Petersburg. Its ranks were so much depleted by sickness and losses in battle that at the end of June, 1864, it was reduced to 145 enlisted men and 11 officers. It took part in the final events that resulted in the surrender of General Lee, and on May 2, 1865, it marched through Richmond. It was mustered out July 13th, of that year.

Among its officers from this county were Col. Alonzo Ferguson of Oneonta, Cleveland J. Campbell of Cherry Valley, adjutant; George W. Ernest jr. of Otsego, quartermaster; William R. Wall of Springfield, captain; Elias Young, first lieutenant; and John Land, second lieutenant of Company D; Edmund C. Gilbert of Butternuts, captain, and Josiah Hinds of Otsego, first lieutenant of Company G; Uriah B. Kendall of Hartwick, captain; William R. Patrick, first lieutenant; William I. Hopkins, second lieutenant of Company H; Alonzo A. Bingham of Otsego, captain; Charles Hamilton of Roseboom, first lieutenant; Edward W. Butler of Roseboom, second lieutenant of Company I. The regiment belonged to the first brigade, second division, second army corps, under the command of General Warren. Of its men, over 400 were from Otsego county.

The Third Calvary, called the "Van Allen Cavalry," in honor of its first Colonel, was composed of men from Otsego, Delaware, Schoharie, and other counties. Its second com-

11

mander was Colonel Simon H. Mix, one of the best officers in the service, who was killed in an engagement on the Weldon railroad. This regiment did good service around Richmond and in North Carolina. It contained 143 men from Otsego county. In July, 1865, it was consolidated with the 1st Mounted Rifles, and designated as the "Fourth Provisional Cavalry."

First Light Artillery.--This regiment was organized at Elmira, but contained 78 Otsego men. Its first commander was Colonel Guilford D. Bailey who was killed at Fair Oaks while spiking some cannon that had to be abandoned to the enemy. He was succeeded by Colonel Charles S. Wainwright, who was promoted to Brigadier General in 1864. This regiment was in battle at Williamsburg, Manassas, Chancellorsville and other places.

Second Light Artillery.--This regiment was organized in New York city, but was largely recruited from the interior of the state, including 150 men from Otsego county. Its battle flag was inscribed with the names of Second Bull Run, Spottsylvania, Cold Harbor, Petersburg, Reams Station and other places.

The Third Light Artillery entered the service as the Nineteenth Infantry Regiment under Col. John S. Clark and was transferred to the Artillery in 1863, and in this capacity served with great credit under Schofield, being attached to the 23rd corps and afterwards on the Atlantic coast, at Hilton Head, Fort Macon, Kingston, Goldsboro, and Charleston. It contained 66 men from Otsego county.

The First Engineer Corps: This was a body of 1,800 picked men from all parts of the country under the command of Col. E. W. Serrell. Companies G and I contained about 100 Otsego men. It was employed in engineer work in Virginia and the Carolinas, and especially in the siege of Forts Sumter and Wagner in Charleston harbor, where it planted the cannon known as the "Swamp Angel" with which the walls of Fort Sumpter were battered down.

## THE G.A.R. POSTS.

There are twelve G.A.R. posts in the county, namely:

Cooperstown, L. C. Turner Post, No. 26.
Cherry Valley, Emory Upton Post, No. 224.
Gilbertsville, W. A. Musson Post, No. 223.
Hartwick, H. N. Duroe Post, No. 653.
Morris, Geo. Kidder Post, No. 61.
Oneonta, E. D. Farmer Post, No. 119.
Otego, C. A. Shephard Post, No. 189.
Portlandville, Olcott Post, No. 522.
Richfield Springs, Weldon Post, No. 256.
Schenevus, Brown Post, No. 15.
Unadilla, C. C. Siver Post, No. 124.
Worcester, Johnson Post, No. 25.

## VILLAGES AND POSTOFFICES.

The following is a complete list of villages and hamlets of Otsego county. There is a postoffice at each place except where some other place is designated. Thus, Bowerstown (mail Cooperstown.)

| Name | Township | Population |
|---|---|---|
| Bourne | Exeter | 20 |
| Bowerstown (mail Cooperstown) | Middlefield | 70 |
| Brighton (mail Richfield Springs) | Richfield | 48 |
| Burlington | Burlington | 111 |
| Burlington Flats | Burlington | 212 |
| Center Valley | Cherry Valley | 107 |
| Chase | Hartwick | 26 |
| Chaseville | Maryland | 123 |
| Clintonville (mail Milford) | Hartwick | -- |
| Cherry Valley | Cherry Valley | 772 |
| Colliersville | Milford | 130 |
| Cooperstown | Otsego | 2368 |
| Cooperstown Junction | Milford | 115 |

13

| | | |
|---|---|---|
| Decatur | Decatur | 91 |
| East Springfield | Springfield | 190 |
| East Worcester | Worcester | 430 |
| Edmeston | Edmeston | 749 |
| Elk Creek | Maryland | 52 |
| Exeter | Exeter | 60 |
| Fly Creek | Otsego | 238 |
| Garrattsville | New Lisbon | 253 |
| Gilbertsville | Butternuts | 476 |
| Hartwick | Hartwick | 605 |
| Hartwick Seminary | Hartwick | 124 |
| Hope Factory (P. O. Index) | Otsego | 130 |
| Hyde Park (mail Index) | Hartwick | 150 |
| Ketchum | Pittsfield | 19 |
| Laurens | Laurens | 233 |
| Lena | New Lisbon | 15 |
| Lentsville | Middlefield | 36 |
| Maple Grove | Morris | 44 |
| Maple Valley | Westford | 29 |
| Maryland | Maryland | 227 |
| Middlefield | Middlefield | 243 |
| Middlefield Center | Middlefield | 108 |
| Middle Village (mail E. Springfield) | Springfield | 60 |
| Milford | Milford | 532 |
| Milford Center (mail Portlandville) | Milford | 100 |
| Monticello (P.O. Richfield) | Richfield | 218 |
| Morris | Morris | 553 |
| Mount Vision | Laurens | 300 |
| New Lisbon | New Lisbon | 169 |
| North Edmeston | Edmeston | 15 |
| Oaksville | Otsego | 149 |
| Oneonta | Oneonta | 7147 |
| Oneonta Plains (mail Oneonta) | Oneonta | 100 |
| Otego | Otego | 658 |
| Otsdawa | Otego | 62 |
| Patent | Burlington | 23 |
| Phoenix Mills | Middlefield | 150 |
| Pierstown (mail Cooperstown) | Otsego | 75 |
| Pittsfield | Pittsfield | 73 |
| Plainfield Center | Plainfield | 32 |
| Pleasant Brook | Roseboom | 127 |

14

| | | |
|---|---|---|
| Portlandville | Milford | 352 |
| Richfield Springs | Richfield | 1537 |
| Roseboom | Roseboom | 226 |
| Salt Springville | Cherry Valley | 119 |
| Schenevus | Maryland | 613 |
| Schuyler Lake | Exeter | 406 |
| Snowdon | Otsego | 27 |
| South Edmeston | Edmeston | 206 |
| South Hartwick | Hartwick | 63 |
| South Valley | Roseboom | 227 |
| South Worcester | Worcester | 150 |
| Springfield | Springfield | 160 |
| Springfield Center | Springfield | 350 |
| Stetsonville (mail New Lisbon) | New Lisbon | 40 |
| Toddsville | Hartwick | 302 |
| Unadilla | Unadilla | 1172 |
| Unadilla Center | Unadilla | 73 |
| Unadilla Forks | Plainfield | 312 |
| Welcome | New Lisbon | 13 |
| Wells Bridge | Unadilla | 165 |
| West Burlington | Burlington | 110 |
| West Edmeston | Edmeston | 222 |
| West Exeter | Exeter | 167 |
| Westford | Westford | 167 |
| West Laurens | Laurens | 117 |
| West Oneonta | Oneonta | 207 |
| Westville | Westford | 72 |
| Wharton | Burlington | 26 |
| Worcester | Worcester | 1020 |

## PATRONS OF HUSBANDRY.

This organization has fifteen local societies or granges in Otsego county. Its objects are educational, financial and social. It insures farm property, advocates good roads, and has been influential in the establishment of free-rural mail delivery. Meetings are held every two weeks for the discussion of topics pertaining to the interests of farmers. The states gives to each grange, on application, an agricultural library of 100 volumes. The membership in Otsego county

15

numbers 665 and consists of farmers and their families. The first grange in this county was organized at Elk Creek in 1886 and since that date W. H. Chamberlain of Elk Creek has been county deputy and secretary.

## SUMMER RESORTS.

The high altitude and salubrious climate of Otsego county render it an attractive region for summer residence. Richfield Springs has long been a favorite health resort, and Cooperstown, with its surroundings, famous as the scene of the "Leatherstocking Tales," will never lose its charm while "Glimmerglass" invites the wanderer to its placid waters. But while these two places are most noted there are many others where summer dwellers find coolness, health and rural beauty. With its increased railroad facilities, which already link together its most attractive spots, Otsego county, with its fifty-three villages, so long isolated from the outer world, is now accessible from all directions, and no small portion of its prosperity is due to its easy communication with the great cities to which it sends its abundant dairy and other products and from which it receives in summer many seekers of rural peace and pleasure.

## THE OTSEGO SOCIETY.

The natives of Otsego county, however far they may roam, never forget the old home and do much to perpetuate the memory of it. Those who dwell in and near New York city have organized a society containing now 66 members, the purpose of which is thus set forth in its constitution: "The society is organized for the purpose of establishing a closer intimacy among the present residents of New York city and vicinity who have come from the county of Otsego, and for the purpose of cultivating social intercourse among its members."

The society was organized February 26, 1901, with the Hon. Silas B. Dutcher of Brooklyn, a native of the town of Springfield, as president and Edwin J. Johnson esq. of Brooklyn, a native of Richfield, as secretary.

# PART II--THE TOWNSHIPS

-------

# BURLINGTON

-------

*Area 27,217 Acres. Population 1,263.*

BURLINGTON was formed from the township of Otsego in 1792 and was then much larger than at present, Pittsfield and Edmeston having since been set off from it. The surface consists chiefly of hilly uplands and ridges extending north and south, which at various points, attain an elevation of 400 feet above the valleys. The principal streams are Butternuts and Wharton creeks.

The early settlers of the township came mostly from Vermont, but some from Massachusetts and Connecticut. In 1787 came the five Angel brothers, Jonathan, William, Joseph, James and Thomas, and in 1789 Captain Gad Chapin, and Perez Briggs. In 1790 came Alexander Parker, Deacon Benjamin Herrington with his four brothers, Elijah, Francis, Richard and Elisha; the four Johnson brothers, Elisha, Harris, Ira and John, and the three Church brothers, Amasa, Willard and Cady. About this time came Jedediah Peck, a leading citizen who represented the county in the state legislature from 1799 to 1804. He is honorably remembered as the author of the bill establishing the public school system of the state. Other honored names in the early days were Jeremiah and Elisha Pratt, Samuel Gardner, Lemuel Hubble, Uriah Balcom and Zacheus Flint.

Other respected families of the olden time, whose names have been perpetuated, are those of Deacon Albert Bolton, and his son Daniel, Colonel David Gardner, Dan Mather and his son Andrew A. Mather, Lemuel Bolton and his family of ten children, Capt. Elisha Parker, a soldier of the Revolution and Roswell Kelsey.

17

Caleb Clark, formerly president of the First National Bank of Edmeston, approaches his nineth year at his home in West Burlington, or with his grandchildren in Oneonta, with a cheerfulness that is an explanation of his long life.

Burlington is a prosperous agricultural town. The leading industry is dairying, the milk being mostly sent to the local cheese factories, or to the Borden condensery at Edmeston.

VILLAGES: There are three villages in this township, viz.: Burlington (population 111), Burlington Flats (population 212) and West Burlington (population 110). Wharton and Patent are rural post offices.

SCHOOLS: Number of districts 13. Teachers 14. Children of school age, 214.

CHURCHES: There are six churches in the township, viz.: At Burlington, Baptist and United Presbyterian; at West Burlington, Episcopal and Methodist; at Burlington Flats, Baptist and Methodist.

# BUTTERNUTS

-------

*Area 26,008 Acres.  Population, 1,698.*

UTTERNUTS was formed from Unadilla in 1796.  Its surface is a hilly upland rising from the Unadilla river, which bounds it on the west, in a series of steep bluffs to the height of 500 or 600 feet.  Butternuts Creek flows southwest through a deep valley near the center of the town. A large number of smaller streams flow through valleys among the hills, dividing the ridges and giving to the region a peculiarly broken appearance.

Gilbertsville, formerly called Butternuts, is the only village in the township.  The following graphic description of it is abridged from a sketch published in the local paper, the *Otsego Journal.*  "The village is located in a beautifuly valley. On the west a high hill rises abruptly.  Downward through the hills extends a deep ravine into which a little brook flows, in springtime rushing down with the violence of a mountain torrent and in summer rippling gently over the stones on its way throughthe heart of the village.  Toward the east the valley stretches away for some distance.  Through this valley flows the Butternuts Creek on its winding course.  This stream is spanned in three places at roads leading directly into the village by iron bridges.  On the hill just south of the village are situated the fine residences of Thos. Swinyard and N. C. Chapman, who make Gilbertsville their summer home. The site of the village was included in the Patent of 35,000 acres of land granted by the state to Lewis and Richard Morris as indemnity for property destroyed during the Revolution.  The name Butternuts was derived from the descriptions in the Morris and Wharton Patents, all beginning at "Three Butternut Trees" growing from one stump or root. The Messrs. Morris divided their Patent by lot.  General Jacob Morris received from his father, Lewis Morris, a tract of 5,000 acres.

"Abijah Gilbert of Warwickshire, England, came to America in 1786, spending the winter with relatives in New

Jersey. It was here he met Richard and Lewis Morris and purchased a tract of 1,000 acres for which he paid 571 pounds, 8s, 8d. before seeing the wilderness that was to become his home. The original tract included the portion where Gilbertsville now stands, reaching away through the Butternuts valley and back on the hills bounding the village. In 1787 Gen. Jacob Morris made his first expedition into the region accompanied by Mr. Gilbert, and the settlement of the village began in the same year.

"The second settler was Joseph Cox, also of Warwickshire, England. The third settler was a woman, Betsy Nichols, and the first wedding that which celebrated her marriage with Joseph Cox. Mr. Cox introduced the making of English cheese, still quite an industry in that section. Dairying is the principal occupation at the present time.

"In those early days the timber being so abundant was of comparatively little value. The main object of work was to clear the land for crops. The fourth immigrant was John Marsh, an energetic young pioneer from Connecticut. He brought a yoke of oxon of great service in logging. In 1791 Mr. Gilbert returned to England and in the following spring brought his family to the log cabin home in America.

"Two sons of Abijah Gilbert, John Y. and Joseph T., who had been attending school at Schenectady, came to the settlement in 1799. About the same time came also William Musson and Samuel Cotton, with whom Mr. Gilbert formed a business partnership under the name of Musson, Cotton and Gilbert. This firm established a store on the Musson farm in 1806. Religious services were held for some time in Mr. Gilbert's barn, and the first religious society was formed in 1797."

Edward Thorp was a pioneer north of the village. His son Henry was a member of Assembly in 1873. Charles Root, the father of Major Charles P. Root, was an early settler in the eastern part of the township. The Shaw brothers, Deacon Samuel, Col. David and William came from Massachusetts in 1796.

Other pioneers who are honarably remembered were Capt. John Bryant, and the brothers, Levi and Thomas Halbert. Levi Halbert was the first teacher in the town. The first supervisor was Lewis Franchot (1796-'98), and the first town clerk Hezekiah Dayton (1796-1805).

SCHOOLS: Number of districts, 15. Number of teachers, 15. Children of school age, 320.

The Gilbertsville High School occupies the substantial stone building formerly used by the Academy. It is under the control of the Regents of the University of the State, and grants Regents' diplomas. It provides a classical course of four years. It is well supplied with apparatus, maps, and anatomical models. Pupils have access also to the excellent village library. The faculty of the school consists of a principal and four assistants.

CHURCHES: At Gilbertsville, Baptist, Episcopal, Methodist, and Presbyterian.

NEWSPAPERS: The *Otsego Journal*, published at Gilbertsville. Established 1876.

# CHERRY VALLEY

-------

*Area, 24,058 Acres. Population, 1,802.*

CHERRY VALLEY township was organized in 1789 and then comprised all that portion of the county east of Otsego Lake and the Susquehanna river, and including the whole of the present town of Springfield, but with the increase of population it was repeatedly subdivided until eight townships had been formed from the original one.

The surface is generally hilly. The highest elevations in the county are in this township, several points exceeding 2,000 feet in height. Among these is Mount Independence, three miles east of Cherry Valley village, and formerly regarded as the highest, but the New York State Survey has recently determined a higher point, namely a hill two and one-fourth miles northwest of Centery Valley on which a signal station of the survey has been established. This summit is 2,301 feet above tide, and is the highest known point in the county.

The waters of the central and southern part flow into the Susquehanna, while the northern part is drained by tributaries of the Mohawk. The soil is fertile, particularly in the valleys, where are found many of the finest farms in the county.

The village of Cherry Valley is beautifully situated on Cherry Valley creek near the centre of the township, and is romantically environed by hills. It was the first white settlement in the county, dating from a land grant made by the authorities of New York to John Lindesay and others in 1738, the settlement being made two years later. Its name was derived from the abundance of wild cherries that grew in the vicinity.

The early history of this place is of unusual interest and importance. It has been given in part in connection with the general history of the county. The massacre of 1778 desolated the place. A few brave settlers remained under the protection of the garrison, which was called away the next summer; but a second surprise and massacre by the savages

22

in the spring of 1780 (eight being killed and fourteen carried into captivity), caused the unfortunate settlement to be completely abandoned.

"It was indeed wiped out of existence, all that remained--the fort, the church, and every dwelling being burned, and thus the results of the labors of nearly forty years were destroyed and the valley returned into the undisputed possession of the beasts and the birds, and Cherry Valley, a few years before the largest and most prominent of the frontier settlements of New York, was but a name." (Sawyer's History, page 41.)

But with the return of peace the settlers who had survived the horrors of war and massacre returned and sought their former homes, though they found only a wilderness, but the hardships they had endured fitted them for their new struggle. The village rose from its ruins and its builders were soon re-inforced by the western tide of emigration of those days, and in a few years Cherry Valley was again the largest settlement south of the Mohawk.

In 1783 General Washington, accompanied by Governor George Clinton and other distinguished men, being on an extended tour through the state, visited Cherry Valley. The party was entertained at the house of Col. Samuel Campbell. Judge William W. Campbell (a grandson of Samuel), in his "Annals of Tryon County," relates the following incident of this visit. Gov. Clinton, observing several stout boys, remarked that they would make fine soldiers sometime. Mrs. Campbell replied that she hoped the country would never need their services. "I hope so, Madam," said Washington, "for I have seen enough of war."

Cherry Valley has been the birthplace or residence of some distinguished men, among whom are the following:

Col. Samuel Campbell, a distinguished patriot of the Revolution and one of the heroes of the battle of Oriskany, where he took the chief command after Gen. Herkimer was wounded.

Col. Samuel Clyde, also one of the heroes of the battle of Oriskany and of the border wars of the Revolution. He was the first sheriff of Otsego county.

Rev. Dr. Eliphalet Nott, president for sixty years of Union College, Schenectady, whose first pastorate was at Cherry Valley.

Hon. William W. Campbell, Justice of the Supreme Court of New York, and author of "Annals of Tryon County," "Life of DeWitt Clinton," and other works.

Hon. Jabez D. Hammond, an eminent lawyer, Otsego County Judge, Member of Congress, author of "Political History of the State of New York," and "Life and Times of Silas Wright."

Hon. Levi Beardsley, lawyer, State Senator, and author of "Beardsley's Reminiscences," a valuable contribution to local history.

Dr. Joseph White, an eminent physician and surgeon, president of the Otsego Medical Society, of the New York State Medical Society, and of the Fairfield Medical College. He was almost equally distinguished in law and in finance, a man of wonderfully varied attainments.

Rev. Solomon Spaulding, the first principal of Cherry Valley Academy and the reputed author of the "Book of Mormon," which he wrote as a romance.

Other noted men of the early time were the lawyers Alvin Stewart, James O. Morse, James Bracket, Isaac Seeley, George Clyde and Horace Lathrop. The Cherry Valley bar was famous throughout the state. Sawyer says in his history: "The history of this country, and probably of the whole world, presents no other case in which a village of less than a thousand people has possessed, at one time, so great an array of local talent, in active and successful practice."

Among the early settlers who are honorably remembered were also Archibald McKellip, James Thompson, James Cannon, William Peeso, Dr. David Little, Major John Walton, Robert Shankland, a native of Ireland and a famous patriot and Indian fighter, James and John Wilson and Edwin Judd.

An old lady, writing of the early times in Cherry Valley, related the following of Alvin Stewart, the wittiest and most successful lawyer of his time in the state: "He was a teacher at first in the Academy, and always kept his eyes open when he made the prayer at the opening of the school. One scholar, bolder than the others, said: 'Mr. Stewart, why do you always keep your eyes open when you pray?' He said, 'we are commanded to watch as well as pray.' But he was much liked by his pupils. I wish I could remember all the funny things I've heard of him. An old lady told me that once a boy did something against the rule, and he told him to go and get some withes. When the boy came back he told him he thought he should have to kill him; and, as he threatened, he kept poking the withes in the ashes to season them. When school was dismissed, he took up the bundle of sticks and told the boy to run; and he whipt all the benches and chairs, and the boy escaped unscathed. He was addicted to taking too much sometimes, but he afterwards reformed and became a great temperance man."

VILLAGES: This township contains three villages, viz.: Cherry Valley (population, 772); Salt Springville (population, 119), and Center Valley (population, 107).

SCHOOLS: Number of districts in the township 12. Number of teachers 16. Children of school age 295.

The Cherry Valley High School is the successor of the famous old Cherry Valley academy. It is a Regents' school of high grade, with a wide range of scientific and classical instruction. The building has recently been enlarged, improved and supplied with new apparatus. The library contains 1,500 volumes.

CHURCHES: There are four churches: Baptist, Episcopal, Methodist Episcopal and Presbyterian.

NEWSPAPERS: The *Cherry Valley Gazette*, one of the oldest papers in the county (established 1818), is the local organfor Cherry Valley and admoining townships.

# DECATUR

-------

*Area, 12,841 Acres. Population, 559.*

DECATUR township was set off from Worcester in 1808. Its surface is hilly, broken by narrow valleys. The principal streams are Oak and Parker creeks tributary to the Schenevus. The first settlement was made in 1790 by Jacob Kinney near the present village of Decatur. The first merchant in the village was Nahum Thompson, who was member of the assembly in 1844. The first supervisor was David Tripp, and the first town clerk was Lemuel Fletcher.

The first school was taught by Samuel Thurber about the year 1798.

The first grist mill was erected by John Champion, the grandfather of S.B. Champion, editor of the *Stamford Mirror.* James Stewart built the first carding mill.

Jacob Brown and his son Jacob came from Columbia county in 1787. Nathan and Gardner Boorn were early settlers. Amos, a son of Gardner, was supervisor for six years. The brothers, Elisha, John and Samuel Waterman, came from Norwich, Connecticut, soon after the Revolution. From Elisha was descended the late Lewis Edson Waterman, the inventor of the "Waterman Ideal Fountain Pen." Mr. Waterman was born in Decatur in the year 1837, and died in Brooklyn, N.Y. in 1900.

Other pioneer settlers were John Treat, Charles Treat, Charles Kaple, Orra Ferris, Amos Crippen, Robert Lansing, Chelsea and Lorenzo Dow Davis and Andrew Sloan.

VILLAGES: This is a strictly agricultural township, having only one village, Decatur, with a population of 70.

CHURCHES: There is only one church in the township. a Methodist church at the village of Decatur.

SCHOOLS: Number of districts, 6. Number of teachers, 6. Children of school age, 75.

# EDMESTON

-------

*Area, 27075 Acres.  Population, 1,767.*

EDMESTON was formed from the town of Burlington in 1808.  The surface is an elevated upland, broken by numerous valleys.  The highest elevations are about 400 feet above the Unadilla river which forms its western boundary.  The township takes its name from Col. Edmeston, an officer in the old French war (1754-1763), who for his services received from the crown a tract of 110,000 acres along the Unadilla river.  To this tract Col. Edmeston sent Persifer Carr, a faithful old soldier of his command, who remained here until carried away with his family captive by the Indians, but after the Revolution he returned.

In 1818 William Stickney and Samuel Simons built a forge and trip hammer for the manufacture of axes, rifle barrels, scythes and wroght iron plow shares.  The first physician was Dr. Gaines Smith, who came with his family from Vermont in 1800.  His grandson, Hon. David B. St. John, became a resident of the town in 1820.  Other early settlers in the town who have living descendants were David Chapin, with his large family, Nathan Langworthy, Henry D. Crandall, Stephen Hoxie, Adin and Lyman Deming, John S. Coon, Charles F. Goodrich, Levi D. Banks, Daniel R. Barrett, Abel Matterson, Charles Burlingham, Erastus Waldo, Daniel R. Barrett, Joseph Bootman, James P. Ackerman, Ephriam Chamberlain, Edwin Phelps, John T. Richards, Hiram Wright, Benjamin Peet, George B. Talbot, Elder Taylor, Andrew Hawkins, Silas Coates, Julius Lines, Samuel Hopkins, O. L. Smith, George Arnold, Daniel Chapin and Jacob Talbot.

VILLAGES:  There are three villages in this township: Edmeston (population 749), West Edmeston (population 222), and South Edmeston (population 206).

SCHOOLS:  Number of districts, 13.  Number of teachers, 17.  Children of school age, 266.

The Edmeston High School is under the supervision of the Board of Regents.  The academic department has a well equipped laboratory, a library of 1,000 volumes, and all necessary reference books. The faculty consists of a principal and four assistants.

CHURCHES: There are six churches in the township of Edmeston, namely: Baptist, Methodist and Free Methodist at Edmeston village; Baptist and 7th day Baptist at West Edmeston and a Union church at South Edmeston.

NEWSPAPERS: The *Edmeston Local*, established in 1882, circulates also as a local organ in the townships of Burlington, Pittsfield, Plainfield, and New Lisbon.

# EXETER

-------

*Area, 11,895 Acres.  Population 1,087.*

EXETER was formed from Richfield in 1799. The surface is generally hilly, some of the elevations being 300 feet above the valleys. It is drained by Herkimer and Sutherland creeks which flow into Canadarago lake and by Butternuts and Wharton creeks which flow into the Unadilla river.

The earliest landed proprietors in this township were Major John Tunnicliff and William Angell. Major Tunnicliff was a gentleman of intelligence, culture and wealth, who came from Derby, England, in the year 1756, and purchased 12,000 acres of land belonging to the patent that had been recently granted to David Schuyler and others, his purchase lying to the west of Fly Creek and being mainly within the present township of Exeter but extending somewhat into Richfield. Here he built a cabin at a place called "The Oaks," and commenced a settlement, but danger from the Indians soon caused him to abandon it until the close of the French war, when he returned with his family and made here his permanent home.

William Angell was from Rhode Island and located on what has since been known as Angell's Hill, in school district No. 3. His family consisted of six sons and several daughters. His son William G. Angell was an influential man, and represented his district in congress.

Other early settlers were Jonathan Angell, Seth Tubbs, Jacob Goble, Caleb Clark, Bethel Martin, Amos and Hull Thomas, Joshua Gorton, Uriel Stone, Ashel Williams and Augustus Curtiss. John and Aaron Phillips of Cambridge, Mass. came to Exeter in 1790. They established a circulating library, and in 1822 a Congregational church. Among the early settlers was Hon. Levi Beardsley, an eminent lawyer and author of "Beardsley's Reminiscences and Ancedotes." He came to Exeter in his infancy with his parents in 1790. The family settled on "The Herkimer Farm," but afterwards removed to Richfield.

## A PIONEER HOME IN THE FOREST.

To give an idea of the trials endured by the settlers in those days we quote from his entertaining book of "Reminiscences:"

"We left our eastern home with a cart, one or two wagons, one or two yoke of oxen, three or four horses, and a few cattle, sheep, and hogs. The roads were excessively bad, and we took but little household goods with us. My mother was left behind with a sick child. My sister, about two years younger than myself, was with me, stowed in a cart or wagon among the chairs and furniture, and put under the care of a girl brought up by my grandfather."

Some distance this side of Canajoharie they abandoned their vehicles, in consequence of the bad roads, and proceeded on their journey. "Some of the party drove the live stock, and went on the best way they could. My father put a saddle on one of the horses, and on another packed a bed and bedding, on which the girl was to ride. I was placed on the horse behind him, on a pillow tied to the saddle, with a strap under my arms buckled to his waist to prevent me from falling off, and carrying my sister before him we pursued our journey, the girl Sukey, riding the other horse on top of the bed and bedding, and a yearling colt tagging after. This constituted the cavalcade, so far as my father and his family were concerned."

Their destination was finally reached, and soon after Mr. Beardsley's father returned to the east and brought his wife and sick child to the new country. He says:

"She rode the horse on a man's saddle, and carried the child, my father in a patriarchal manner walking by her side; and thus the family were at last re-united in the woods at the foot of the beautiful lake, and by the side of the fine little stream known as Herkimer creek, then full of fish, particularly the speckled trout.

"This house that we moved into was a small log cabin, the body laid up, and part, though not the whole, of the roof covered with black ash and elm bark, which had been peeled

30

from the trees at the season when bark is taken off easily. When opened out and put on the roof and pressed down with poles or small timbers, the rough side exposed to the weather, it makes a good roof that will last several years and shed the rain quite well. The house was only partially covered, and when it rained we had to put our effects and ourselves under that part which was sheltered.

"The floor was of basswood logs, split and hewed partly on one side, and then spiked down making a substantial floor, but only about half was laid. We had no fire place or chimney, and till this was built the cooking must all be done out of doors.

"A mud-and-stack chimney and fireplace were afterwards added as the weather became cold, and to get earth or clay to make mortar to daub the house and make the chimney, a hole was dug under the floor which was our only cellar, in which, in winter, we put a few bushels of potatoes and turnips, and took up one of the flattened logs from the floor whenever we wanted something from below. I have said there was no door when we moved in. My father on reaching the house with my mother and family, suspended a blanket at the doorway to keep out part of the night air."

## THE FIRST WEDDING.

Mr. Beardsley gives a further insight into the customs of those days in his description of the first wedding. He says:

"Let me describe the first wedding, which was the marriage of a sister of my mother, who was married to Ebenezer Russell: the marriage was at my father's, in the log house. I do not remember how the parties were dressed, but no doubt in their best gear. Judge Cooper, of Cooperstown, was sent for, being the nearest magistrate, and came eighteen miles principally through the woods, to perform the ceremony. The neighbors were invited, the old pine table was in the middle of the room, on which I recollect was placed a large wooden bowl filled with fried cakes (nut cakes or donughts, as the country people call them). There might have been something else to constitute the marriage feast, but I do not recollect anything except a black junk bottle filled with rum; some maple sugar and water. The judge was in his long riding boots, covered with mud up to his knees, his horse was fed, that he might be off when the ceremony was over. The parties presented themselves, and were soon made man and wife as his "Honor" officially announced. He then gave the bride a good hearty kiss, or rather smack, remarking that he always claimed that as his fee; took a drink of rum, drank health, prosperity and long life to those married, ate a cake or two, declined even staying to supper, said that he must be on his way home, and should go to the foot of the lake that night, refused any other fee for his services, mounted his horse and was off; and thus was the first marriage celebrated."

VILLAGES: There are three villages in this township, viz.: Schuyler Lake (population 406), West Exeter (population 167) and Exeter (population 60).

SCHOOLS: Number of school districts, 8. Number of teachers, 11. Children of school age, 158. The Union Free School at Schuyler Lake employs four teachers and is well organized for efficient work.

CHURCHES: There are five churches in this township, viz.: at Exter, Methodist; at West Exeter, Methodist; at Schuyler Lake, Baptist, Methodist and Universalist.

# HARTWICK

-------

*Area, 25,980 Acres.   Population, 1,800.*

HARTWICK was formed from Otsego in 1802. Its surface is hilly, the highest summits being 200 to 350 feet above the valleys. It is drained by several small streams that flow into the Susquehanna and the east branch of the Otego creek. The township was named in honor of the Rev. John Christopher Hartwick who, in 1752, purchased from the Indians for the sum of 100 pounds, a tract of land embracing nearly all of the present township and amounting to 21,500 acres. Mr. Hartwick was a native of the dukedom of Saxe-Gotha in the province of Thuringia in Germany, and had come as a Lutheran missionary to this country. He was for many years a noted preacher throughout the country from New England to Virginia, and it was not until after the Revolution that he settled down upon his purchase and established a colony. Through the agency of Judge William Cooper he let a great part of his land to settlers at an annual rental of one shilling per acre, with the privilege of purchasing at fourteen shillings per acre.

HARTWICK SEMINARY. In his will Mr. Hartwick left his whole fortune for the establishment of the Seminary that bears his name. The school was opened on the 15th of December, 1815, with the Rev. Dr. Ernest Lewis Hazelius as principal. It now has three departments--Regents, Collegiate and Theological. The buildings have recently been remodeled and enlarged. The institution is located four miles south of Cooperstown, on the Cooperstown and Charlotte Valley railroad.

Conspicuous among the natives of Hartwick was William H. Bissell who was born in this town in 1811, but early removed with his parents to Milford where he grew to manhood. He prepared himself for the medical profession, but abandoned it for the law. In 1837 he removed to Illinois, from which state he served as a colonel in the Mexican war. He also represented his district in congress from 1849 to

1855. In 1856 he was elected governor of the state, was re-elected and died at Springfield, Ill. in 1860, while serving his second term.

Among the early settlers were the brothers John and Nathan Davidson, William and Nathan Field, Jerry Potter, Jedediah Ashcraft, Joseph Marsh, Nicholas and Rufus Steere, Amos and Joseph Winsor, Benjamin and Nicholas Camp, John and Philip Wells, Hopkins Burlingham, Isaac Bissell, Deacon Ziba Newland, Amasa Peters, Uriah Luce, Stephen Ingalls, David and Josiah Maples, Daniel Murdock and Col. Henry Wheeler. The first supervisor was Philip Wells, and the first town clerk was Rufus Steere who built the cotton factory at Toddsville.

VILLAGES: There are five villages in this township, viz.: Hartwick (population 605), Hartwick Ceminary (population 124), South Hartwick (population 63), Toddsville (population 302), and Hyde Park (population 150). Chase is a rural postoffice. Clintonville, formerly a cotton cloth manufacturing village, has now only an electric lighting plant, from which Cooperstown is supplied, postoffice at Milford. On the Fourth of July, 1902, Hartwick village celebrated its 100th anniversary.

SCHOOLS: Number of districts, 16; number of teachers, 17; number of children of school age, 342. The Hartwick Union Free school has a commodious building, newly furnished and provided with a good library, natural history and chemical apparatus, and other appliances for teaching. It is a school of four grades and confers Regents' diplomas on its academic graduates.

CHURCHES: There are eight churches in this township, viz.: At Hartwick, Baptist, Christian and Methodist; at Toddsville, Union and Methodist; at Hartwick Seminary, Lutheran; at Hyde Park, Methodist; and a Christian church near Christian Hill in the northern part of the township.

NEWSPAPERS: There are two weekly papers, the *Hartwick Review* and *Hartwick Visitor*, published at Hartwick village. The *Hartwick Seminary Monthly and Eastern Lutheran*, the organ of Hartwick Seminary, is edited and published at the Seminary.

# LAURENS

-------

*Area, 26,116 acres. Population, 1,483.*

AURENS was formed from Otsego in 1810. Otego creek, the principal stream, flows nearly south through a fertile and well cultivated valley. The first white settler within the present limits of the town was Joseph Mayall. He located in 1773 about one mile north of the present village. He was a man of great courage, and during the Revolution was celebrated as an Indian fighter. In the same year Richard Smith came from Baltimore and erected a fine colonial mansion, called "Smith Hall," one and a half miles north of the village. It has recently been purchased and restored by Willard V. Huntington esq. An early settler was the Quaker, John Sleeper, who maintained a peaceful neutrality during the Revolution, though for a time compelled to leave on account of danger from the Indians. He reared here a family of seven sons and five daughters.

The day before the massacre of Cherry Valley, Mr. Sleeper started for New Jersey, and upon arriving at Cherry Valley was urged by his friends to remain over night. But he declined and continued his journey to Bowman's creek, several miles distant, and thereby saved his life.

The day following the massacre, a party of savages passed through Laurens and robbed the family of Mr. Sleeper and burned their buildings. Brant, the Indian chief, arrived soon after and, finding Mrs. Sleeper still there, exclaimed, "My God! Mrs. Sleeper, are you alive?" She replied: "Yes; but they have destroyed all of our property." Brant charged the destruction upon the Senecas, saying: "They would kill their best friends," and offered to pay her for the loss, but Mrs. Sleeper, being of the Quaker faith, refused, as she believed that he had come wrongfully by it. The family soon after returned to New Jersey suffering terribly on the way.

At the close of the Revolution Mr. Sleeper returned with his family and rebuilt the house and mill. In 1794 he sold his grist and saw mills and 1,000 acres of land to Griffin

Craft of Cherry Valley, who was the first supervisor of the town in 1811.

In 1813 General Erastus Craft succeeded to his father's estate. He was a member of assembly in 1810, '13 and '14, and served as supervisor of the town for thirteen years. He married a sister of Judge W. W. Campbell of Cherry Valley and has descendants in this vicinity and in the west. Other early residents were General William Comstock, a leading merchant, William C. Fields, who represented his district in congress in 1866, General William Armstrong, Erastus and Ezra Dean, Chauncey Strong, Samuel Allen, Jacob Butts, Nathan Newell, Cyrus Hudson, Solomon Harrison, Peter Scramling, Calvin Straight, a Quaker preacher, Solomon Eldred, Rufus Steere, Stephen Whipple and Joshua Matteson.

Rufus Tucker and Daniel Weatherly were early settlers at West Laurens. Dr. Ezer Windsor settled above Laurens on the Mount Vision road in 1794. His son Amos was sheriff in 1842.

Thomas Keys came with his large family from Connecticut in 1805. His descendants are influential citizens at Oneonta and elsewhere.

VILLAGES: There are three villages in this township, viz.: Laurens (population 233), Mt. Vision (population 300), and West Laurens (population 117). Otsego Park, near Laurens village, on the line of the O.C.&R.S. electric railway, eight miles from Oneonta, is a new and popular pleasure resort.

CHURCHES: There are three churches in the village of Laurens, viz.: Methodist, Christian and Presbyterian; at Mt. Vision, Baptist and Methodist; at West Laurens, Christian and a Friends meeting house.

SCHOOLS: Number of districts, 12; teachers, 14; children of school age, 265.

Laurens village has an efficient school of eight grades, with two teachers and 80 pupils. It has a library and school apparatus and prepares for Regents' examinations.

NEWSPAPERS: *The Otego Valley News*, a weekly paper is published at Laurens. Established, 1899.

# MARYLAND

-------

*Area, 29,873 Acres. Population, 1,998.*

**T**HIS township was formed from Worcester in 1808.
The principal stream is the Schenevus creek, which
flows south-west through the town and empties into
the Susquehanna.

The surface consists chiefly of a hilly upland, broken
by ravines. The settlement of the town dates back to 1790,
at which time Elisha Chamberlain and the three brothers,
Israel, Elephas and Phineas Spencer, located near the present
Maryland station on the railroad. The first settlers where
Chaseville is now located were Jotham Houghton and his two
sons Jerehamel and Daniel. Daniel was a captain in the war
of 1812. Wilder, Ezekiel and John Rice settled near Schenevus, Caleb Boynton in the eastern part of the town, and
Joseph Howe in Elk Creek. Early settlers and large land
owners were Josiah Chase and John Bigelow, who came in
1791 and purchased 1,000 acres of land. In 1794 arrived
many pioneers, prominent among whom were John Thompson and his sons John and James from Columbia county.
They located near the foot of Crumhorn Mountain and their
descendants have been leading citizens.

Other settlers in the vicinity of Elk Creek were Earl
Wright, Philemon Perry, Eleazer Grove, John Kelly, and the
Chase brothers, Asa, Dean, Seth and John, with their
families.

One of the first necessities of the early time was a grist
mill near at hand. For a long time all grain had been sent to
Cherry Valley. There was, therefore, great rejoicing when in
1794, those enterprising pioneers, Israel and Elisha Spencer,
erected a mill near the present Maryland railroad station. At
about the same time Jonathan Houghton built a saw mill
near Chaseville, but afterwards removed it to a place near
Spencer's Mills. These mills were built by Phineas Spencer,
the pioneer carpenter. He was a mechanical genius. He
made furniture, plows and coffins. For years he made all the

37

burial cases free of charge. They were doubtless made, as was the custom in those days, of pine boards, colored black by a solution of water with the ashes of straw.

The first death in the town was that of the wife of Josiah Chase. The remains were borne a distance of seven miles to the Maryland cemetery, the bearers being on foot as was the custom, for this was regarded as more respectful to the dead.

VILLAGES: There are four villages in this township, viz.: Schenevus (population 613), Maryland (population 227), Chaseville (population 123) and Elk Creek (population 52).

The Schenevus Valley Fair is held annually on the spacious grounds near Schenevus village.

SCHOOLS: Number of districts, 15; teachers 23; children of school age, 481. The Schenevus High school is under the board of Regents, and is well equipped for efficient work. It is supplied with apparatus for the teaching of the natural sciences, with maps, globes, charts, reference books and a circulating library of 1,000 volumes. A Regents' diploma corresponding to an Academic course of four years is conferred upon its graduates.

CHURCHES: At Schenevus, Baptist, Catholic, Episcopal, and Methodist. At Maryland, Christian and Lutheran. At Chaseville, Baptist. At Elk Creek, Methodist.

NEWSPAPERS: At Schenevus, the *Schenevus Monitor*, a weekly paper, established in 1863.

# MIDDLEFIELD

-------

*Area, 37,456 Acres. Population, 2,100.*

MIDDLEFIELD is the largest township in the county. It was set off from Cherry Valley in 1797. The surface is hilly, the summits being 400 to 500 feet above the valleys. It is well watered by the Cherry Valley and Red creeks, which flow into the Susquehanna.

The first settlement was made at Newtown-Martin, now Middlefield (locally Clarksville), about 1760; but during the Indian wars of the Revolution the place was exposed to great danger, and all the more so on account of the patriotic spirit that sent its best men to the Continental army. The town was, in the end, completely depopulated, but at the close of the war its fertile lands were rapidly taken up by old and new settlers, among whom were William Cook, the four McCollum brothers; Reuben Beals, Bernard Temple, Gardner Blair, Levi H. Pierce, John Parshall, David Anderson, Benjamin Gilbert, James Bradley, Capt. Thomas Ransom and Major Jothan Ames.

VILLAGES: There are three villages in this township, viz.: Middlefield (population 243), Middlefield Center (population 108) and Phoenix Mills (population 150). Lentsville is a rural postoffice. Bowerstown is a hamlet (population 70), with postoffice at Cooperstown. Westville is partly in Middlefield, with postoffice and churches in Westford. The "Index Knitting Mills," at Phoenix Mills, employ (including branch at Hope Factory), about 400 hands.

The County Poor House and Farm are situated in this township, on the railroad, three miles south of Cooperstown.

SCHOOLS: Number of districts, 19. Teachers, 18. Children of school age, 322. The village schools are graded and efficiently conducted.

CHURCHES: There are three churches in this township, viz.: At Middlefield, Baptist and Methodist; at Middlefield Center, Presbyterian.

# MILFORD

-------

*Area, 28,172 Acres. Population, 2,007.*

THIS township was formed from Unadilla in 1796. The surface is a hilly upland, divided into two ridges by the Susquehanna river, which flows through it in a southerly direction. The declivities are in many places very steep. Crumhorn mountain, on the east border, attains an elevation of 600 feet above the valley.

The fertile soil and excellent water power afforded by the rivers early attracted settlers to this region. Among the leading families at Milford village were those of Charles Morris and his sons Richard and David, James Westcott, John Aylesworth, Norman Bissell, Levi Hungerford and Jonathan Sweet; at Portlandville, Thomas Mumford, Russell Briggs and Col. John Moore, the Edsons at Edson Corners, and at Colliersville Isaac Collier, his son Major Peter Collier, and his son-in-law, Jared Goodyear.

VILLAGES: There are four villages in this township, viz.: Milford (population 532), Portlandville (population 352), Colliersville, (population 130), and Cooperstown Junction (population 115). Milford Center (population 100) is a hamlet with rural free delivery from Oneonta.

SCHOOLS: Number of districts 14; number of teachers, 13; children of school age, 290. The Milford High School is under the Regents, and is efficiently organized in all departments. A specialty is made of commercial training and business practice. The faculty consists of a principal and five assistants.

CHURCHES: At Milford village, Presbyterian and Methodist; at Portlandville, Christian, Episcopal and Methodist; at Cooperstown Junction, Methodist; at Milford Center, Baptist.

NEWSPAPERS: The *Otsego Tidings* and *Teachers' Gazette* at Milford village.

# MORRIS

-------

*Area, 24,035 Acres.    Population, 1,689.*

T̲HERE were early settlements in this region, but the present township was not organized until 1847, when it was set off from Butternuts. The surface is varied and attractive, rising in broken uplands from the fertile valley of the Butternuts creek, which receives numerous brooklets. The western ridge terminates in a steep bluff bordering on the Unadilla river.

The township derives its name from General Jacob Morris, a son of Lewis Morris, who was a signer of the Declaration of Independence, and who, with his brother Richard, received a patent of 30,000 acres of land in this vicinity to indemnify them for the loss of property destroyed by the British during the Revolution.

An early and influential settler was Mr. Paschal Franchot, a native of France, who raised here a family of ten children. His son Richard was one of the leading men of his time in the county. He was supervisor of the township, representative in the Congress, first colonel of the 121st New York regiment in the rebellion, and the first president of the Albany and Susquehanna railroad. Other early settlers whose names have been perpetuated are Ebenezer Knapp, Benjamin Stone, Jeremiah Cruttenden, Jonathan and Ansel Moore, Amos, Jacob & Ichabod Palmer, Benjamin Lull with his five sons, Benjamin jr., Joseph, Caleb, Nathan and William, Dr. William Yates, and Ziba Washbon.

Some of the customs of those days are thus described by the late Ashel S. Avery of Morris, in his contribution to Hurd's history of the county: "It was a common thing for a shoemaker (cobbler) to 'whip the cat,' that is, go into a farmer's house, put his kit in the corner of the room, and with one last, made perhaps from a stick off the wood-pile, make the shoes for the whole family--the largest first, then cutting down the last to the next smaller size, the farmer

41

furnishing the leather. 'Rights and lefts' shoes were unknown. The shoe pegs were all made by hand.

"In the square-room of well-to-do people were brass-ornamented andirons in the fire-place. In the summer time this fire-place would be filled with sparrow-grass (asparagus); but after wall paper became cheap, fire-boards, with a landscape on them, filled up the space. It was a great invention when the tin baker was made; quite an improvement on the bake-kettle, or the board on which the Johnny-cake was baked before the fire.

"One stage coach ran from Cooperstown to Oxford three times a week. It was a four-horse yellow coach, and looked, in the children's eyes, as large as a circus does now-a-days. The postmaster could have carried any one mail in his hat. The postage on a letter was as follows: To Garrattsville, 6 cents; to Cooperstown, 10 cents; to Albany, 12 1/2 cents; to New York, 18 3/4 cents; and to Philadelphia, 25 cents. There were no envelopes; the sheet of paper was folded up so as to tuck one edge into another, and sealed with a wafer or sealing wax."

VILLAGES: There is only one village in this township, viz.: Morris (population, 553). Maple Grove is a hamlet on the southern border (population 44). South New Berlin, on the river, is mostly in Chenango county.

Morris has always been one of Otsego's pleasantest villages. One of the best and best attended annual fairs of the county is that held here by the Butternuts Valley Agricultural Society.

SCHOOLS: Number of districts, 12; teachers, 16; children of school age, 295. The Morris High School is the oldest union free school in the county. In its building and equipment it ranks among the best. Its academic department fits for either normal school or college, and also for professional schools of law and medicine. Its faculty consists of a principal and five assistants.

CHURCHES: At Morris, Baptist, Episcopal (with "Morris Memorial Chapel"), Friends, Methodist, and Universalist; at Maple Grove, Episcopal.

NEWSPAPERS: The *Morris Chronicle*, at Morris.

# NEW LISBON

-------

*Area 26,899 Acres. Population, 1,225.*

THIS township was organized in 1806. Among the earliest settlers were Elnathan Noble from whom Noblesville was named. Increase Thurston, Linus N. Chapin, a surveyor, Joseph Neff, a famous violinist, Elias Cummings, William Gregory, Amos Perry, John Cope and Remington Kenyon, Benjamin Cutler, a soldier of the war of 1812, came from Vermont in 1799. He died in Mt. Vision in 1871, at the age of 101 years and five months.

Garrattsville was named for John Garratt. He and his wife were carried into captivity by the Indians and held by them seven years. It is related that when they saw the Indians approaching their cabin, Mrs. Garratt seized her clock and silverware and fled out the back door, concealing the silver under an inverted pig trough, while the clock was hastily thrown over the garden fence. After an absence of seven years they returned to find their clearing covered with underbrush and weeds, but there, under the pig trough, was found the silver, and down by the garden fence the old clock.

VILLAGES: Garrattsville (population 253), and New Lisbon, formerly Noblesville (population 169). Lena and Welcome are rural postoffices. Stetsonville is a hamlet with a postoffice at New Lisbon.

SCHOOLS: Number of districts, 16; number of teachers, 16; children of school age, 263.

CHURCHES: At Garrattsville, Methodist, United Presbyterian, and an Episcopal Mission; at Welcome, Baptist; at New Lisbon, Episcopal.

# ONEONTA

-------

*Area, 21,930 Acres.  Population, 8,910.*

THIS township was formed from portions of Milford and Otego in 1830.  The Susquehanna river flows through the southern part, dividing it into two ridges.  The hills south of the river, called South mountain, attain an elevation of about 700 feet above the valley, and 1,800 feet above sea level.  The center and northern part of the township is hilly and broken by the Otego, Silver, Oneonta and Emmons creeks.  It was a favorite resort of the Indians in the olden time, and the present Main street is believed to be on the line of an Indian trail.

Of white settlers, previous to the Revolution, little is known.  The names of Scramling, Young and Alger are all that have come down to us from that time.  General Sullivan's destructive expedition in 1789 broke the power of the aborigines, and after the war the tide of emigration was early turned to this attractive region.

Among the early families were those of Henry Scramling, Frederick Brown, Abram Houghtailing, William Morenus, Peter Swart, James Young, Jacob Wolf and his son Conradt, John and Nicholas Beams, Frederick Bornt, David Alger, Elihu Gifford and his seven sons, Solomon Yager and his son David, Josiah Peet, Ira Emmons, and Dr. Joseph Lindsay, who was the first physician.

Jacob VanWoert settled at the mouth of Otego creek, Andrew Parish, James Blanchard and Thomas Morenus on the south side near "Round Top."  Col. William Richardson built a saw and grist mill on Oneonta creek in the vicinity now known as "Richardson Hill."

At Emmons, on Emmons creek, then a place of some importance, Major Asa Emmons built a carding and fulling mill.  At Oneonta Plains early settlers were Elisha Shepherd and Asel Marvin.

VILLAGES:  There are two villages in this township,-- Oneonta, with a population of 7,147, and West Oneonta, population 207. The plain west of Oneonta village, in the triangle between the rivers, is called Oneonta Plains. It has a considerable settlement, and a Methodist church. Postoffice, Oneonta.

SCHOOLS: Number of districts, 14; number of teachers, 38; children of school age, 1,683.

CHURCHES: There are thirteen churches in this township, viz.: At Oneonta, Baptist, Free Baptist, Catholic, Christian Science, Episcopal, Methodist, Presbyterian, United Presbyterian and Universalist; at West Oneonta, Baptist and Free Baptist; at Oneonta Plains, Methodist, and a Methodist church at Richardson Hill.

NEWSPAPERS: There are six newspapers published in Oneonta, viz.: The daily *Star*, and the following weekly papers: the *Herald*, the *Lender*, the *Press* and the *Spy*. The *Oneontan* is a monthly and is issued during the school year as the organ of the State Normal school.

## ONEONTA VILLAGE.

The village of Oneonta is pleasantly situated on the north bank of the Susquehanna river, and on the line of the Delaware and Hudson railroad, nearly midway between Albany and Binghamton, 82 miles from Albany and 61 miles from Binghamton. The greater part of the village lies upon a gentle slope that rises from the river for nearly a mile to the northward, and affords from its summit a commanding view of the village and of the wooded highlands that surround it in nearly every direction.

Oneonta is a growing and prosperous village, and is becoming a railroad and manufacturing center of considerable importance. Its railroad connections are the extensive "Delaware and Hudson" system, the "Ulster and Delaware," extending from Oneonta to Kingston on the Hudson, the "Cooperstown and Charlotte Valley" road, which crosses the "Delaware and Hudson" near the village, and the "Oneonta, Cooperstown and Richfield Springs" electric railroad, which is to connect at Herkimer with the "New York Central."

The "Delaware and Hudson" railroad shops at this point employ nearly 600 men, and the enlargement of the plant, now in process of construction, will materially increase

45

this form. Other important industries are the "Oneonta Milling Company," the "Paragon Silk Mills," the branch of the "Gloversville Knitting Company," the "Buckley Shirt Manufactory," the "Dauley & Wright Marble Works," and the extensive cigar manufactories of Doyle & Smith, and Hayes & Bowdish.

The wholesale trade of Oneonta is important, especially in the lines of flour and grain, groceries, crockery, glassware and paper. The "Central New York Fair" is held here each year in the month of September, and is always largely attended.

The "Oneonta Building and Loan Association" contributes to the establishment of homes by its stock loans to members. A state armory is located here, and an efficient military organization maintained (Company G, 1st Reg't. N.G.N.Y.).

The buildings of the State Normal School, which was established here in 1889, occupy a commanding position upon the eminence at the northern side of the village. It is one of the best equipped and most successful Normal schools of the state. Other institutions and societies are the "Aurelia Osborn-Fox Memorial Hospital Society," the "Young Men's Christian Association," the "Oneonta Club," and the "Woman's Club."

The village is lighted by electricity, has an excellent water supply, complete telegraph, telephone and express service, and the principal business streets are well paved. The electric road extends through the village to the East End suburb, with a branch to the normal school.

THE VILLAGE SCHOOLS.

The Union Free school, which dates from 1867, employs a superintendent and twenty-three teachers, and has 1,125 pupils enrolled. The High School department, under the Regents, fits for college or business. It is well supplied with apparatus, charts and specimens for the study of the natural sciences. Its business course includes book-keeping, commercial law, typewriting and stenography. With this school will always be associated the memory of the late Nathaniel N. Bull, for twenty-five years it efficient and much esteemed principal (1870-1895).

The East End suburb, population 564, has a graded school that employs three teachers. It has a new and commodious school building.

# OTEGO

-------

*Area, 26,534 Acres.   Population 1,817.*

HIS township was organized from parts of Unadilla and of Franklin, Delaware county, in 1822, and then called Huntsville. In 1830 the name was changed to Otego. The settlement commenced soon after the Revolution. Among the first were Ransom Hunt, of Bennington, Vt., Capt. Peter and Col. Elisha Bundy, Capt. Elisha Saunders, Deacon Lester Newlands, John, Michael and Nathan Birdsall, Benjamin Edson, a soldier of the Revolution, John Blakely, Rowland Carr, John A. and Andrew Hodge, Michael and Benjamin Shepherd, Sylvester Goodrich, John and Nahum Smith, Thurston Brown, Benjamin Estes, James Wait and Daniel Weller.

The population in the early days was, as in Oneonta, a mixture of New Englanders and Mohawk Germans, and much rivalry and frequent fights occurred until chosen champions, John French for the "Yankees," and Peter Scramling for the "Dutch," settled it at a sawmill raising on the premises of Ransom Hunt.  The Yankee was the victor, and so peace was established.  At Otsdawa early settlers were Frederick Martin, Nathan Emerson, King Hathaway and Henry Sheldon.

VILLAGES:  There are two villages in this township, Otego, (population 658), and Otsdawa (population 62).

SCHOOLS:    Number  of  districts,  18;  number  of teachers, 20; children of school age, 319.  The Union Free school at Otego, under the Board of Regents, is well organized for efficient work in all departments.  The building has lately been remodeled and provided with modern furniture and apparatus.  Especial attention is given to vocal and instrumental music.  The faculty consists of a principal and four assistants.

CHURCHES:  At Otego, Baptist, Free Baptist, Episcopal, Methodist, and Presbyterian.  At Otsdawa, Free Baptist.

NEWSPAPERS:  The *Rural Times*, published at Otego.

# OTSEGO

-------

*Area, 32,141 Acres. Population 4,497.*

O TSEGO is the oldest township in the county. It was organized as a part of Montgomery county in 1788, and included nearly all that portion of the present county west of Otsego lake and the Susquehanna river, which rises therein.

Its surface consists mainly of a hilly upland, divided into ridges by Fly and Oaks creeks. The first white man who passed through this region was Cadwallader Colden, surveyor general, in the year 1737. Sixteen years later, in 1753, Rev. Gideon Hawley was sent to this locality as a missionary to the Indians. The next noted visitor was Gen. George Washington, who passed through on an exploring expedition in 1783, and "viewed the Lake Otsego at the source of the Susquehanna."

The Indian wars of the Revolutionary period desolated this whole region, but with the return of peace a tide of emigration set in, and the portion now known as Otsego township was especially attractive.

This influx of settlers dates from 1788. Among the first were William and Asel Jarvis, who became prominent citizens. William was a physician, and Asel erected at Fly Creek, in 1813, the first foundry and machine shop. His three sons, Chester, Dwight and Kent, were leading men and active in the old military organizations. Other early settlers at Fly Creek were John Adams, Ebenezer Cheeney and Oliver Bates.

In 1788 came also George Scoot from Yorkshire, England, and about the same time John Patton from Perthshire, Scotland. Other pioneers were Abner Pier, for whom Pierstown was named, and Major George Pier, a celebrated musician. Hon. Isaac Williams came in 1793. He occupied various important offices. In 1813, 1817 and 1823 he represented his district in congress. Darius Warren came here from Connecticut in 1788, and was the first man who received a deed of land from Judge William Cooper. Erastus

Taylor came from Bennington, Vt., and raised a family notable for longevity.

Other early settlers whose names have been perpetuated in this vicinity are George Roberts, Ira Tanner, Jesse Teft, Norman and Bingham Babcock, Martin Coates, Reuben Hinds, Platt St. John, Andrew Scribner, Levi Pierce, John Badger, Russell Williams, John Baldwin and Eleazur Loomis.

VILLAGES: There are four villages in this township, viz.: Cooperstown (population 2,368), Fly Creek (population 238), Oaksville (population 149), and Hope Factory (population 130). Snowdon and Bourne are rural postoffices.

SCHOOLS: Number of school districts, 18; number of teachers, 32; children of school age, 803.

CHURCHES: There are ten churches in this township, viz.: At Cooperstown, Baptist, Catholic, Episcopal, Methodist, Presbyterian, Universalist. At Fly Creek, Methodist, Presbyterian, and Universalist. In the Hinds neighborhood north of Fly Creek, Methodist.

NEWSPAPERS: *Freeman's Journal, Otsego Farmer,* and *Otsego Republican,* all published at Cooperstown.

## COOPERSTOWN.

Cooperstown was founded by Judge William Cooper, the father of J. Fenimore Cooper, who in 1785 purchased from Colonel George Croghan (who had purchased it from the Indians), a tract of 100,000 acres of land lying on the west side of the river and embracing the site of the present village and extending both north and south of it. He purchased this land before seeing it, but in the fall of the same year, he came with a party of surveyors, and in January, 1786, took formal possession of his property, afterwards known as the "Cooper patent." William Ellison, a surveyor, came the same year, and in 1788, under Mr. Cooper's direction, he laid out the village.

In 1789, a large house having been built for them, Mr. Cooper brought his family from Burlington, N.J., their former home. The youngest member of this company was the child James, aged two years. The name Fenimore, the mother's maiden name, was later added by himself. This child was destined to become the most famous of American novelists, and the place to which he thus came to be famous as the

50

scene of his romantic tales. The following is from a graphic description of Judge Cooper's arrival written in 1871 by G. Pomeroy Keese esq. of Cooperstown:

"One bright October afternoon eighty years ago, as the sun was drawing lengthened shadows over the landscape, bathing in rich autumnal light the hills which surround the limpid waters of Otsego lake, there came around the base of Mount Vision a lumbering family coach, bearing, with its attendant vehicles, the founder of Cooperstown and his household to their new home. All the glorious beauties of the changing foliage which have since charmed so many thousands who have visited this still rural retreat, were in their virgin splendor, and as the new comers looked upon the scene and beheld in the reflection of the lake below the dark shades of the evergreens contrasted with the gold and crimson hues of the maple and the beech, they must have been sadly insensible to the chief attraction of their future abode if they failed to see in it one of the most perfect combinations of hill and valley, lake and forest, which the hand of painter could portray. The party, numbering fifteen in all, with the family domestics, was an imposing cavalcade in this primitive region just emerging from the wilderness . .
. The whole population of the place--thirty-five in all--were drawn up to receive the 'lord of the manor,' who, from henceforth, as the first judge of the county and its largest landed proprietor, became the leading spirit of all that region."

The village thus began more than a century ago, although of slow growth, has always prospered and kept pace with modern progress. Its streets are broad and well kept; its driveways along the lake and river delightful, and its camping and boating facilities unsurpassed. It has an electric lighting plant, is supplied with pure water, and its spacious hotels and dwellings invite summer guests, of whom a great number are received every season. The work of the public authorities has been generously supplemented by Mrs. Alfred Corning Clark, a distinguished resident, to whom the place in indebted for a beautiful park and gymnasium, and for the splendid edifice of the Young Men's Christian Association.

To its natural beauty of situation and its advantages as a summer resort, Cooperstown adds the romantic interest that is associated with the "Leatherstocking Tales." Cooper excelled in his descriptions of natural scenery, and the reader who bears his vivid pictures in mind will easily recognize the localities along the lake made classic by his genius.

Cooperstown has been at times the permanent or summer home of some famous men, among whom, beside the great novelist, are Samuel F. B. Morse, Thurlow Weed, Gen. John A. Dix, Abner Doubleday, Gen. George C. Starkweather, Hon. Samuel Nelson, Justice of the United States Supreme Court, and Col. William L. Stone, editor of the *New York Commercial Advertiser.*

The Otsego County Agricultural Society holds an annual fair at Cooperstown, which is largely attended.

Important benevolent institutions at Cooperstown are the "Thanksgiving Hospital," in the establishment of which Miss Susan Fenimore Cooper, a daughter of the novelist, was largely instrumental, and the "Orphan House of the Holy Savior," which is under the control of the Episcopal diocese of Albany, but which receives inmates regardless of denominational lines.

## THE COOPERSTOWN HIGH SCHOOL.

This institution is fully equipped for thorough instruction. It is supplied with all needed apparatus, and with a library of 4,000 volumes. The academic department, under the Regents, prepares for college and for law and other special courses. The faculty consists of a principal and eleven assistants.

## COOPER'S GRAVE AND MONUMENT.

James Fenimore Cooper died at his home in Cooperstown on the 14th of September, 1851, at the age of sixty-two years. Cooper sleeps in the churchyard beside his kindred, an unpretending slab marking the site of his grave. His monument is at Lakewood cemetery, on the eastern shore of the lake, just beyond the site of the panther scene in the "Pioneer." It is of Italian marble, twenty-five feet high, with a figure of Leatherstocking on the summit. Natty is represented as loading his rifle and gazing off on the lake spread out beneath him, while his dog by his side watches his master with eager interest.

# PITTSFIELD

-------

*Area, 22,584 acres. Population, 1,101.*

ITTSFIELD was formed from Burlington in 1797. It retained its original dimensions until 1806, when the present town of New Lisbon was set off from it. It consists mainly of fertile uplands laying between the valley of the Unadilla river, which constitutes its western boundary, and the Butternuts creek valley on the east. Some of the earliest settlers came from Pittsfield, Mass., and hence the name. Among them were Dr. Joseph O. Cone, Capt. Aaron Noble and Samuel Tyler. The two latter settled at Pittsfield village, locally called Pecktown, from Alvin Peck, who kept the hotel there.

Capt. Abel DeForest, a soldier of the Revolution, was an early settler at Meeker Hill. Gardner Hall came from Pownal, Vt. in 1797. His son, William G. Hall, became the leading physician of the town. Seth Harrington and Benjamin Eddy settled in the eastern part about 1793. Jabez Beardsley was a prominent settler in the western part on the river. He was supervisor for eleven years. Capt. Joseph Briggs, another veteran of the war, came early from Vermont. He and his son Silas were prominent citizens. Other early settlers were Augustus and Gardner Sheldon, Ezekiel Chapin and Stephen Hawkins.

This is a prosperous agricultural township and is chiefly devoted to dairying, the milk being sent either to the condensery at New Berlin or to the shipping station at Edmeston. It contains one village, Pittsfield, with a population of 70, and a rural postoffice at Ketchum.

SCHOOLS: Number of districts, 12; teachers, 10; children of school age, 189.

CHURCHES: There is a Union church at Ketchum, Ebenezer Chapel in the southern part is supplied by the Baptist and Methodist pastors from Morris.

# PLAINFIELD

-------

*Area, 17,142 acres.  Population, 897.*

PLAINFIELD was set off from Richfield in 1799.  The surface is hilly, the bluffs along the Unadilla river, which constitutes its western boundary, rising to the height of 400 feet.  The first settlement was made in 1793, and the first settlers were Luther Smith, Elias Wright, Giles Kilbourne, Ruggles Spooner, Samuel Williams, Benjamin and Abel Clark.  Among the most useful pioneers was Caleb Brown, who built the first grist mill in the town at "The Forks."  He also built an oil mill and cloth factory on the east branch of the Unadilla, and a woolen factory a short distance south of the Forks.

A noted family was that of Parley Phillips, who came from Massachusetts prior to 1800, and raised here a family of twelve children.  Joshua Babcock and his nine children were also prominent in the olden time.  He was a member of the assembly in 1818 to 1821, and presidential elector in 1836.  Azariah Armstrong came from Vermont in 1812.  He had nine children, several of whom have been leading citizens.

At Plainfield Center Joseph Sims was an early settler.  His son Jeptha was the author of "Sims' Border Wars."  Joseph Sims jr., a grandson of Joseph, was a noted author and lecturer.

VILLAGES:  This is a fertile and prosperous township chiefly devoted to dairying.  It contains only one village, Unadilla Forks, with a population of 312. Plainfield Center is a hamlet, the seat of a Welch colony that still preserves its native language. Leonardsville is mostly in Madison county.

SCHOOLS:  Number of districts, 11; teachers, 8; children of school age, 131.  There is a Union Free school at Unadilla Forks with three departments.

CHURCHES:  At Unadilla Forks, Baptist and Free Baptist.  At Plainfield Center, Welch Congregational, with preaching in the Welch language.

55

# RICHFIELD

-------

*Area, 20,418 acres.   Population, 2,526.*

THIS township was formed from Otsego in 1792. It then included the townships of Exeter and Plainfield, which were set off from it in 1799.  The surface is rolling and moderately hilly with a mean elevation of 150 to 200 feet above Canadarago (or Schuyler) Lake.   Several wooded mountain peaks near the eastern boundary rise 300 feet higher.   Canadarago Lake, the northern portion of which is within this township, lies in a deep valley and is fed by a number of streams which enter it from the northwest.   Its outlet is Oaks Creek, through which its waters flow southward into the Susquehanna river.   The settlement of this region was rapid as soon as the close of the Indian wars made it safe to establish homes in the wilderness.   The northern portion of Otsego county was regarded with especial favor in consequence of its beautiful lake scenery, fertile soil, good timber and eligible millsites and water privileges.

The most important landed proprietor who located here in the early times was John Tunnicliff of Derby, England, who, in 1756, purchased 12,000 acres belonging to the Otsego patent.  In the year 1774 he made a further purchase of 600 acres from the Schuyler patent, this purchase including a portion of the present village of Richfield Springs.

### RICHFIELD SPRINGS.

The springs that have made this locality famous as a health resort were long known to the aborigines under the name of "Medicine Waters." The following beautiful description is given of the original spring and of Canadarago Lake: "At the summit of a gently-rising eminence in the mist of shrubbery, and overshadowed by the lofty and majestic branches of the fir and pine, there issued forth from beneath the roots of a gigantic tree a crystal mineral fountain of life and health.  About three hundred rods to the south of this fountain was a romantic and beautiful lake silently sleeping in a quiet valley, skirted on either edge by heavily-wooded alpine ranges, whose giant forest trees were boldly reflected in the deep blue waters that were disturbed only by the screaming waterfowl or the light canoe of the red man as he glided swiftly over its silver surface. The elk, moose and timid deer drank from its silent waters in the wild solitudes of the primeval forest. Two wood-covered islands rested within the bosom of this picturesque lake, one of which has since disappeared, and, as tradition says, the last of the once powerful tribe, the Canadaragos, sank with it far beneath its dark waters."

From the discovery of these springs and their preparation for public use by Dr. Horace Manley in 1820 the village dates its fame as a watering place. The efficacy of the waters was found to be very great in the treatment of many forms of disease and with every returning season the number of visitors increased.

"The location of Richfield Springs is remarkable for natural beauty, not only in its immediate surroundings, but it occupies a position in the midst of the most charmingly diversified mountain and lake scenery. The mountain sides, in many instances, and especially where bordering upon lakes and streams, are jutted with immense ledges of rocks, or cut with deep ravines that assist in giving that romantic character to this portion of the state of New York which it so eminently possesses. Six beautiful lakes are distributed in this vicinity, almost within sight of each other. This was a region of popular resort of the aboriginal tribes of the valley of the Mohawk and western part of the state before he whites encroached upon it."

To the natural advantages so plain to the red man the white brother has added those of art and culture. Electricity illuminates the streets and pure water from a mountain lake finds its way to the dwellings. Railroad connection is now perfect on the north with the "Delaware, Lackawanna and Western" and the "New York Central," to the south with the "Delaware and Hudson" system by way of Cooperstown and Oneonta.

VILLAGES: There are two villages in this township, viz.: Richfield Springs (population 1,537) and Monticello

57

(population 218).  Brighton is a hamlet with postoffice at Richfield Springs.

SCHOOLS:  Number of districts, 11; number of teachers, 20; number of children of school age 558.

The Richfield Springs Union Free school has an excellent building and is supplied with modern apparatus, charts, natural history specimens and a circulating library of 1,000 volumes.  The academic department, subject to the visitation of the regents, awards classical and scientific diplomas and has also a commercial course and a teachers' training class.  The faculty consists of a principal and twelve assistants.  Total attendance about 450.

CHURCHES:  There are nine churches in this township, viz.: At Richfield Springs, Catholic, Episcopal, Methodist, Presbyterian and Universalist.  At Monticello, Baptist, Episcopal and Universalist.  At Brighton, Methodist.

NEWSPAPERS: At Richfield Springs are published the *Richfield Springs Mercury*, weekly and the *Richfield Springs Daily*, during the months of July and August.

# ROSEBOOM

-------

*Area, 19,739 Acres. Population, 1,031.*

ROSEBOOM was formed from Cherry Valley in 1854. The surface is diversified, many of the hills rising to the height of 350 feet above the valleys. It is embraced in the original grant to John Lindesay, and was divided into the Belvidere, McKean, Long, and Beaver Dam patents. This was the last town organized in the county and was named in honor of Abram Roseboom, who with John Roseboom owned, at the beginning of the century, a tract of 2,000 acres lying in the present towns of Middlefield, Cherry Valley and Roseboom.

For many years the mercantile business of the locality was conducted at Cherry Valley, and it was not until 1832 that a store was opened within the present limits of the town. This was kept by Daniel Antisdel at Lodi (now Roseboom). The first grist mill was built by Cornelius Low in 1818.

Among the early settlers were John Boyce, William Pesco, Simeon Rich, John and Peter Sutphen, Smith Hull, Peter Low, Daniel Clark, Solomon Coats, Rufus Perkins, John Pearson, and Isaac Keeling. Some of the early residents are now living at a great age. Mrs. Mary (Keeling) Pearson at Pleasant Brook is ninety-five, Mrs. Lucy Boyce at Roseboom is ninety-three, and Dr. John W. Sterriker of Roseboom is eighty-seven.

This is a prosperous agricultural township. The leading industry is dairying, the milk being sent to cheese factories.

VILLAGES: Roseboom (population 226), South Valley (population 227), and Pleasant Brook (population 127), Lowell's Corners is a hamlet on the eastern border.

SCHOOLS: Number of districts, 12; teachers, 11; children of school age, 148.

CHURCHES: At Roseboom, Baptist and Methodist, at South Valley, Methodist, Methodist Protestant and Christian;

at Pleasant Brook, Methodist and Methodist Protestant; at Bentley Hollow, Methodist Protestant.

# SPRINGFIELD

-------

*Area, 26,522 Acres.  Population, 1,762.*

SPRINGFIELD was set off from Cherry Valley in 1797. The surface is a rolling upland.  A promontory east of the head of Otsego Lake, called Mt. Wellington, rises to a height of 400 feet.  It is a prosperous agricultural township.

In the year 1762 five families took up lands in the town, viz.: those of John Kelly, Richard Ferguson and James Young in the eastern part, Gustavus Klumph and Jacob Tynart at the head of the lake. Very few additions were made to this little community until after the Revolution.  At the battle of Oriskany in 1777 Capt. Thomas Davy, who has descendants now living in the town, was killed.  In the following year Joseph Brant, the leader of the Six Nations, came to Springfield with a party, burned the town and killed or carried into captivity the men, but this famous chief was merciful.  It is recorded that he "gathered together the women and children into one house and left them injured--an act not followed by his tory allies."

On the return of peace there was an immediate influx of settlers into this region.  Among them were Benjamin Rathbun and John Cotes, who as a lad of sixteen had taken part in the battle of Bunker Hill, John James and Robert Young.

Other pioneers after the Revolution were Moses Franklin, Abner Cooke, Calvin and Luther Smith.  Elisha Hall, the inventor of the well known Hall threshing machine, was a pioneer at Springfield Center. Hezekiah Hayden was a pioneer and his descendants have been distinguished elsewhere.

VILLAGES:  Springfield (population 160), Springfield Center (population 350) and East Springfield (population 190).  Middle Village is a hamlet with postoffice at East Springfield.

SCHOOLS:  Number of districts, 13; teachers, 16; children of school age 309.

61

CHURCHES: At Springfield Center, Baptist, Episcopal and Universalist; at East Springfield, Episcopal, Methodist and Presbyterian.

# UNADILLA

-------

*Area, 28,349 Acres. Population, 2,601.*

THIS township was formed from Otsego in 1792. It lies at the confluence of the Susquehanna and the Unadilla, and is watered by the many tributaries of these rivers. It is believed to have been settled to some extent before the Revolution, but where or by whom is not known. Like all other parts of the country, it filled up rapidly as soon as peace permitted.

Unadilla village dates from about 1790, but its early importance was due to the construction in 1802 of the Catskill and Susquehanna turnpike, an important highway which terminated here, the point being known as "Wattles' Ferry," from Sluman Wattles, a leading pioneer in that region. The village was on lands of the "Wallace patent." Among the first settlers were Aaron Axtell, the village blacksmith, who purchased the first lot; Solomon Martin, a soldier of the Revolution and of the war of 1812, sheriff of the county and member of assembly, from whom Martin brook was named; Daniel Bissell and his kinsman, Guido L. Bissell; Dr. Gordon Huntington, the leading physician of that region and member of assembly from 1805 to 1809; Joseph S. Bragg, whose son Edward S. Bragg, became brigadier general in the Rebellion, and a congressman from Wisconsin; Moses Axtell, one of the "Boston tea party," and a hero of Lexington and Bunker Hill; Stephen Benton, a landholder and merchant; Captain Uriah Hanford, William Wilmot, the first cabinet-maker, Samuel Crooker, the four Cone brothers, Dr. Adanijah, Daniel, Gilbert and Gardner, who, with their descendants, have had an important share in the development of the village; Elisha Luther, John Fiske, a soldier of 1812, Whitney Bacon, David Finch, Henry Ogden, who was member of assembly in 1820, Niel Robinson, John Eells, justice of the peace and supervisor, and Calvin and Lorin Gates, who purchased land here about 1810.

Among influential citizens of a later date were Sherman Page, an able lawyer, member of assembly in 1827, member of the 23rd and 24th congress and associate judge of the county; Major Christopher D. Fellows, who from his advent in the village at the age of fourteen to that of ninety-three, "was an active and intelligent force in nearly all that advanced the interests of the place;" Dr. Gaius Leonard Halsey, author of the "Reminiscenses" included in "The Pioneers of Unadilla," by his son, Francis W. Halsey; Clark I. Hayes, whom farmers have to thank for improved breeds of farm stock throughout this valley; Eli C. Belknap, a leading lawyer; and Arnold B. Watson, than whom no more useful man has ever lived in Unadilla. Alike in educational, religious and financial affairs he was among the first and best.

Ebenezer Gregory came from Gilbertsville to Unadilla Center, where he built the stone house that is still standing. He reared four sons and four daughters, who with their descendants have contributed much to the social and business life of Unadilla.

Among the early proprietors in the vicinity of Sand Hill, in the eastern part of the township, were Daniel Buckley, John and Aaron Sisson, Samuel Merriman and Elisha Lathrop. John Sisson came as early as 1790 and settled in the vicinity afterwards called Sisson Hill. In the same vicinity were captain Seth Rowley, a veteran of the Revolution and Captain Elisha Saunders, who was both physician and soldier, and who was killed at the battle of Queenstown in 1812.

Unadilla is pleasantly situated on the north bank of the Susquehanna river, and on the line of the Albany & Susquehanna railroad, 99 miles from Albany and 44 from Binghamton. It has a superior system of water works, with reservoirs 150 feet above the village, and an electric light plant furnishing 26 arc lights for the streets, with incandescent lights for the stores and dwellings. It is a manufacturing place of some importance, having a large milk condensery, a carriage factory making the superior Hanford carriages and wagons a large tailoring establishment and several cigar factories. It is one of the most attractive villages on the line of the railroad, being noted for its wide and shady streets, its beautiful river view, its handsome residences and its well kept private grounds.

VILLAGES: There are three villages in this township, viz.: Unadilla (population 1,172), Unadilla Center (population 73), and Wells Bridge (population 165). Rockdale, on the Unadilla river, is mostly in Chenango county.

SCHOOLS: Number of districts, 18; teachers, 21; children of school age, 44 [sic]. The Unadilla Union Free School and Academy, which in 1894 succeeded the former academy, has a large, modern building with superior sanitary arrangements, city water and electric lights. It ranks as a High School under the university of the State of New York. Its course of instruction includes the natural sciences, ancient and modern languages, and teachers' training class. It has a library of over 2,000 volumes, besides reference book. The Academic department prepares for college and grants regents' diplomas. The faculty consists of a principal and eight assistants.

CHURCHES: At Unadilla, Baptist, Episcopal, Methodist, and Presbyterian. At Wells Bridge, Baptist and Methodist. At Unadilla Centre, Methodist, and a Methodist church at Sand Hill, in the eastern part.

NEWSPAPERS: The *Unadilla Times*, a weekly paper, established in 1854.

# WESTFORD

-------

*Area, 20,812 Acres.  Population, 910.*

WESTFORD was set off from Worcester in 1808.  The surface is hilly, the summits in many places rising to the height of 250 to 400 feet above the valleys.  It is well watered by the numerous branches of the Elk and Cherry Valley Creeks.

The first settlers came here from Vermont about 1790. They were Thomas Sawyer, Oliver Salisbury, Ephraim Smith, Alpheus Earl, Artemus, Moses and David Howe, and Benjamin Chase, who raised seven sons here.  Robert Roseboom came from New Jersey and located in the northeastern part near Maple Valley.  He was a prominent man and first supervisor of the town, officiating in that capacity until 1814. Samuel and Jonas Babcock, soldiers of the Revolution, came from Berkshire, Mass., in 1795 and their father Josiah joined them in 1799.  The five Sperry brothers gave name to Sperry Hollow.  The Hubbard brothers formed the "Hubbard Settlement" and the Bentley family gave name to "Bentley Hollow." Judge Andrew S. Draper, former State Superintendent of Schools and now president of the University of Illinois, and his cousin, Judge Alden Chester of the Supreme Court, were natives of this township.  Other pioneers were Oliver Bidlake, Joshua and Dexter Draper, David Adams, Eli Tyler, Martin, John and Flavel Wright, Calvin Holmes, James Badeau, Charles Mason, Charles Webster, Eleazer Peasley, Samuel Waterman, Andrew Bice, and Artemas and Jonah Howe, captains of the Revolution.  Westford is a fertile agricultural township largely devoted to dairying.

VILLAGES: Westford (population 167) and Westville (population 72).  Maple Valley is a rural postoffice.

SCHOOLS:  Number of districts, 11; teachers, 10; children of school age, 131.

CHURCHES: At Westford, Methodist, Baptist, Congregational and Episcopal; at Westville, Baptist and Methodist; at Maple Valley, Christian.

# WORCESTER

-------

*Area, 29,030 Acres.   Population, 2,409.*

ORCESTER was formed from Cherry Valley in 1797, and then embraced in addition to its present territory, the towns of Maryland, Decatur and Westford. These towns were set off from it in 1808.  The surface is a hilly upland.  It is fertile, particularly along the Schenevus creek and Charlotte river.  The first settlements were made soon after the Revolution.

Prominent among the pioneers was Silas Crippen.  He was supervisor eight years, justice of the peace, judge of the court, and a member of the state assembly in 1816.  He built, about 1796, the first grist-mill and saw-mill in the town.  His son Phillip was the first white child born in the town.  He had nine other children.   Abram Garfield, the grandfather of President Garfield, lived near Worcester and sleeps in a burial plot now in the heart of the village.

Other pioneers were John Waterman, Henry Stever, Moses Essex, Luther, Lester S. Thomas and Deacon Joseph Flint, Samuel Russ, Jonathan Jennings, Amos Belding, Hazard Smith, Samuel Hartwell, John P. Russ, John Pratt, J. H. Herrington, J. B. Hollenbeck, Green White, John Alvord, David and Alpheus Scott and Philip Becker.   Uriah Bigelow was the first physician in the town.  Abraham Becker, a son of Philip, was a leading lawyer at South Worcester.  A prominent pioneer at East Worcester was John Champion, a native of Connecticut.  At twelve years of age, being too young to carry a musket, he entered the army of the Revolution as a teamster and served in this capacity until the close of the war.  He then married and removed to the town of Worcester, where he settled on what is known as "Elliot Hill," which is now in Decatur.  About 1805 he removed to East Worcester, where he built a grist mill and other buildings.  He raised a family of twelve children, seven sons and five daughters, who have numerous descendants, among them a number of distinguished men. His son Aaron was the father of S. B. Champion, the well known editor of the *Stamford Mirror.*

Among his interesting reminiscences of the early times, Mr. Champion relates the following:

"The first doctor I remember was old Dr. Warner. He was one of the old fashioned kind, and did not believe in people continually pouring down medicine to keep well. He used to say that people doctored too much, as some politicians now say we are governed too much. Near us settled a newly-married couple. The wife was as neat as could be, and everything was in keeping with her personal appearance. Their first-born, a son, was kept, like a doll-baby, in the house. It did not thrive, and Dr. Warner was called in to see it. He looked it over, admired its perfect form and features, took it up and started out of the house with it. The mother was alarmed, and said the doctor would kill it if he did not bundle it up. It was in the spring, and the father of the child was making a garden. The doctor put it down in the newly made onion bed. The baby took up a handful of dirt and commenced eating it. The mother was more frightened, but it was allowed to eat all it wanted. Then the old doctor left them with the remark, "give it plenty of air, for its lungs, clean dirt for its bones, and you will have a large, rosy-cheeked, healthy child, instead of a poor, pale, weakly, emaciated creature."

Other early settlers near East Worchester were Joshua Bigelow, Joseph Bowers, James Lockwood, Isaac Caryl, Adolphus Gott, Calvin Jennings, Cary Pepper and Maj. Gen. James Stewart, whose father, James Stewart, was killed at the battle of Bunker Hill. His son, Dr. William Stewart, was a physician at South Worcester for 60 years.

VILLAGES: There are three villages in this township, viz.: Worcester (population 1,030), East Worcester (population 430) and South Worcester (population 150). Worcester is a flourishing village, provided with electric lights and with pure water from a mountain reservoir 80 feet deep.

SCHOOLS: Number of districts, 15; teachers, 23; children of school age, 470. The Worcester High School, under the Regents, has a modern building, complete scientific apparatus, a thorough academic course and a well selected

68

library. The faculty consists of a principal and seven assistants.

CHURCHES: There are eight churches in the township, viz.: At Worcester, Baptist, Catholic, Congregational and Methodist, at East Worcester, Baptist and Methodist, at South Worcester, Lutheran and Methodist.

NEWSPAPERS: The *Worcester Times*, established 1876, published at Worcester.

# INDEX

## A

Ackerman, James P. 27
Adams, David 66
  John 49
Alden, --- (Col.) 6
Alger, --- 5
  David 44
Allen, Samuel 36
Alvord, John 67
Ames, Jothan 39
Anderson, David 39
Angel, James 17
  Jonathan 17
  Joseph 17
  Thomas 17
  William 17
Angell, Jonathan 29
  William 29
  William G. 29
Antisdel, Daniel 59
Armstrong, Azariah 55
  William 36
Arnold, George 27
Ashcraft, Jedediah 34
Avery, Ashel S. 41
Axtell, Aaron 63
  Moses 63
Aylesworth, John 40

## B

Babcock, Bingham 50
  Jonas 66
  Joshua 55
  Josiah 66
  Norman 50
  Samuel 66
Bacon, Whitney 63
Badeau, James 66

Badger, John 50
Bailey, Guilford D. 12
Balcom, Uriah 17
Baldwin, John 50
Banks, Levi D. 27
Barrett, Daniel R. 27
Bates, Oliver 49
Beals, Reuben 39
Beams, John 44
  Nicholas 44
Beardsley, --- (Mr.) 30, 31
  Jabez 54
  Levi 24, 29
Becker, Abraham 67
  Philip 67
Belding, Amos 67
Belknap, Eli C. 64
Bentley, --- 66
Benton, Stephen 63
Bice, Andrew 66
Bidlake, Oliver 66
Bigelow, John 37
  Joshua 68
  Uriah 67
Bingham, Alonzo A. 11
Birdsall, John 48
  Michael 48
  Nathan 48
Bissell, Daniel 63
  Guido L. 63
  Isaac 34
  Norman 40
  William H. 33
Blair, Gardner 39
Blakely, John 48
Blanchard, James 44
Bolton, Albert 17
  Daniel 17
  Lemuel 17

71

Boorn, Amos 26
  Gardner 26
  Nathan 26
Bootman, Joseph 27
Bornt, Frederick 44
Bowdish, N. 9
Bowers, Joseph 68
Boyce, John 59
  Lucy 59
Boynton, Caleb 37
Bracket, James 24
Bradley, James 39
Bragg, Edward S. 63
  Joseph S. 63
Brant, --- 35
  Joseph 61
Briggs, Joseph 54
  Perez 17
  Russell 40
  Silas 54
Brown, Caleb 55
  Frederick 44
  Jacob 26
  Thurston 48
Bryant, John 20
Buckley, Daniel 64
Bull, Nathaniel N. 46
Bundy, Elisha 48
  Peter 48
Burlingham, Charles 27
  Hopkins 34
Butler, Edward W. 11
Butts, Jacob 36

## C

Camp, Benjamin 34
  Nicholas 34
Campbell, --- 36
  --- (Mrs.) 23
  Cleveland J. 9, 11
  James 4

Campbell, Samuel 23
  W. W. 36
  William W. 23, 24
Cannon, James 24
Carr, Rowland 48
Caryl, Isaac 68
Chamberlain, Elisha 37
  Ephraim 27
  W. H. 16
Champion, Aaron 68
  John 26, 67
  S. B. 26, 68
Chapin, Daniel 27
  David 27
  Ezekiel 54
  Gad 17
  Linus N. 43
Chapman, N. C. 19
Chase, --- 38
  Asa 37
  Benjamin 66
  Dean 37
  John 37
  Josiah 37, 38
  Seth 37
Cheeney, Ebenezer 49
Chester, Alden 66
Church, Amasa 17
  Cady 17
  Willard 17
Clark, Abel 55
  Alfred Corning (Mrs.) 51
  Benjamin 55
  Caleb 18, 29
  Daniel 59
  George 4
  John S. 12
Clinton, --- (Gen.) 6
  George 23
Clyde, George 24
  Samuel 23

Coates, Martin 50
  Silas 27
Coats, Colomon 59
Colden, Cadwallader 49
Collier, Isaac 40
  Peter 40
Comstock, William 36
Cone, Adanijah 63
  Daniel 63
  Gilbert 63
  Gradner 63
  Joseph O. 54
Cook, J. E. 9
  William 5, 39
Cooke, Abner 61
Coon, John S. 27
Cooper, --- 52
  --- (Judge) 31, 51
  J. Fenimore 50
  James Fenimore 52
  Susan Fenimore 52
  William 33, 49, 50
Cope, John 43
Cotes, John 61
Cotton, Samuel 20
Cox, Betsy (Nichols) 20
  Joseph 20
Craft, Erastus 36
  Griffin 36
Crandall, Henry D. 27
Crippen, Amos 26
  Philip 67
  Silas 67
Croghan, George 50
Crooker, Samuel 63
Cruttenden, Jeremiah 41
Cummings, Elias 43
Curtiss, Augustus 29
Cutler, Benjamin 43

# D

Danfort, George E. 9
Davidson, John 34
  Nathan 34
Davis, Chelsea 26
  Lorenzo Dow 26
Davy, Thomas 61
Dayton, Hezekiah 21
Dean, Erastus 36
  Ezra 36
DeForest, Abel 54
Deming, Adin 27
  Lyman 27
Dickson, William 4
Dix, John A. 52
Doubleday, Abner 52
Draper, Andrew S. 66
  Dexter 66
  Joshua 66
Dunlop, Samuel 4
Duroe, H. N. 13
Dutcher, Silas B. 16

# E

Earl, Alpheus 66
Eddy, Benjamin 54
Edmeston, --- (Col.) 4
Edson, --- 40
  Benjamin 48
Eells, John 63
Eldred, Solomon 36
Ellison, William 50
Emerson, Nathan 48
Emmons, Asa 44
  Ira 44
Ernest, George W. 11
Essex, Moses 67
Estes, Benjamin 48

# F

Farmer, E. D. 13
Fellows, Christopher D. 64
Fenimore, --- 50
Ferguson, Alonzo 11
   Richard 61
Ferris, Orra 26
Field, Nathan 34
   William 34
Fields, William C. 36
Finch, David 63
Fiske, John 63
Fletcher, Lemuel 26
Flint, Joseph 67
   Lester S. 67
   Luther 67
   Thomas 67
   Zacheus 17
Franchot, Lewis 21
   Paschal 41
   Richard 10, 41
Franklin, Moses 61
French, John 48

# G

Gallt, William 4
Ganesvoort, Lenelet 4
Gardner, David 17
   Samuel 17
Garfield, --- (President) 67
   Abram 67
Garratt, --- (Mrs.) 43
   John 43
Gates, Calvin 63
   Lorin 63
Gifford, Elihu 44
Gilbert, Abijah 19, 20
   Benjamin 39
   Edmund C. 11
   John Y. 20

Gilbert, Joseph T. 20
Goble, Jacob 29
Goodrich, Charles F. 27
   Sylvester 48
Goodyear, Jared 40
Gorton, Joshua 29
Gott, Adolphus 68
Grant, --- (Gen.) 11
Green, Nelson W. 10
Gregory, Ebenezer 64
   William 43
Grove, Eleazer 37

# H

Halbert, Levi 20
   Thomas 20
Hall, Elisha 61
   Gardner 54
   William G. 54
Halsey, Francis W. 64
   Gaius Leonard 64
Hamilton, Charles 11
Hammond, Jabez D. 24
Hanford, Uriah 63
Hanson, E. N. 9
Harrington, Seth 54
Harrison, Solomon 36
Hartwell, Samuel 67
Hartwick, John Christopher 4, 33
Hathaway, King 48
Hawkins, Andrew 27
   Stephen 54
Hawley, Gideon 49
Hayes, Clark I. 64
Hazelius, Ernest Lewis 33
Herkimer, --- (Gen.) 23
Herrington, Benjamin 17
   Elijah 17
   Elisha 17
   Francis 17

Herrington, J. H. 67
  Richard 17
Hinds, Josiah 11
  Reuben 50
Hodge, Andrew 48
  John A. 48
Hollenbeck, J. B. 67
Holmes, Calvin 66
Hopkins, Samuel 27
  William I. 11
Houghtailing, Abram 44
Houghton, Daniel 37
  Jerehamel 37
  Jotham 37
Howe, Artemas 66
  Artemus 66
  David 66
  Jonah 66
  Joseph 37
  Moses 66
Hoxie, Stephen 27
Hubbard, --- 66
Hubble, Lemuel 17
Hudson, Cyrus 36
Hull, Smith 59
Hungerford, Levi 40
Hunt, Ransom 48
Huntington, Gordon 63
  Willard V. 35

# I

Ingalls, Stephen 34

# J

James, John 61
Jarvis, Asel 49
  Chester 49
  Dwight 49
  Kent 49
  William 49
Jennings, Calvin 68

Jennings, Jonathan 67
Johnson, Edwin J. 16
  Elisha 17
  Harris 17
  Ira 17
  John 17
  William 5
Judd, Edwin 24

# K

Kaple, Charles 26
Keeling, Isaac 59
  Mary 59
Keese, G. Pomeroy 51
Kelly, John 37, 61
Kelsey, Roswell 17
Kendall, Uriah B. 11
Kenyon, Remington 43
Keys, Thomas 36
Kidder, George 13
Kilbourne, Giles 55
Kinney, Jacob 26
Klumph, Gustavus 61
Knapp, Ebenezer 5, 41

# L

Land, John 11
Langworthy, Nathan 27
Lansing, Robert 26
Lathrop, Elisha 64
  Horace 24
Lee, --- (Gen.) 11
Lindesay, John 4
Lindsay, Joseph 44
Lines, Julius 27
Little, David 24
Lockwood, James 68
Loomis, Eleazur 50
Low, Cornelius 59
  Peter 59
Luce, Uriah 34

Lull, Benjamin 5, 41
  Caleb 41
  Joseph 41
  Nathan 41
  William 41
Luther, Elisha 63

# M

Maples, David 34
  Josiah 34
Marsh, John 20
  Joseph 34
Martin, Bethel 29
  Frederick 48
  Solomon 63
Marvin, Asel 44
Mason, Charles 66
Mather, Andrew A. 17
  Dan 17
Matterson, Abel 27
Matteson, Joshua 36
Mayall, Joseph 5, 35
McCollum, --- 39
McKellip, Archibald 24
Merriman, Samuel 64
Mix, Simon H. 12
Moore, Ansel 41
  John 40
  Jonathan 41
Morenus, Thomas 44
  William 44
Morris, Charles 40
  David 40
  Jacob 19, 41
  Lewis 19, 20, 41
  Richard 19, 20, 40, 41
Morse, James O. 24
  Samuel F. B. 52
Mumford, Thomas 40
Murdock, Daniel 34
Musson, W. A. 13

Musson, William 20

# N

Neff, Joseph 43
Nelson, Samuel 52
Newell, Nathan 36
Newland, Ziba 34
Newlands, Lester 48
Nichols, Betsy 20
Noble, Aaron 54
  Elnathan 43
Nott, Eliphalet 24

# O

Ogden, Henry 63
Olcott, Egbert 9, 10

# P

Page, Sherman 64
Palmer, Amos 41
  Ichabod 41
  Jacob 41
Parish, Andrew 44
Parker, Alexander 17
  Elisha 17
Parshall, John 39
Patrick, William R. 11
Patton, John 49
Pearson, John 59
  Mary (Kelling) 59
Peasley, Eleazer 66
Peck, Alvin 54
  Jedediah 17
Peeso, William 24
Peet, Benjamin 27
  Josiah 44
Pepper, Cary 68
Perkins, Rufus 59
Perry, Amos 43
  Philemon 37
Pesco, William 59

Peters, Amasa 34
Phelps, Edwin 27
Phillips, Aaron 29
  John 29
  Parley 55
Pier, Abner 49
  George 49
Pierce, Levi 50
  Levi H. 39
Potter, Jerry 34
Pratt, Elisha 17
  Jeremiah 17
  John 67

# R

Ramsay, David 4
Ransom, Thomas 39
Rathbun, Benjamin 61
Reynolds, --- (Gen.) 10
Rice, --- 10
  Ezekiel 37
  John 37
  Wilder 37
Rich, Simeon 59
Richards, John T. 27
Richardson, William 44
Roberts, George 50
Robinson, Niel 63
Root, Charles 20
  Charles P. 20
Roseboom, Abram 59
  Jacob 4
  Robert 66
Rowley, Seth 64
Russ, John P. 67
  Samuel 67
Russell, Ebenezer 31

# S

Salisbury, Oliver 66
Saunders, Elisha 48, 64

Sawyer, Thomas 66
Schramling, Henry 5
Schuyler, David 29
Scoot, George 49
Scott, Alpheus 67
  David 67
Scramling, Henry 44
  Peter 36, 48
Scribner, Andrew 50
Seeley, Isaac 24
Serrell, E. W. 12
Shankland, Robwert 24
Shaul, John D. 9
Shaw, David 20
  Samuel 20
  William 20
Sheldon, Augustus 54
  Gardner 54
  Henry 48
Shephard, C. A. 13
Shepherd, Benjamin 48
  Elisha 44
  Michael 48
Simons, Samuel 27
Sims, Jeptha 55
  Joseph 55
Sisson, Aaron 64
  John 64
Siver, C. C. 13
Sleeper, --- (Mrs.) 35
  John 35
Sloan, Andrew 26
Smith, Calvin 61
  Ephraim 66
  Gaines 27
  Hazard 67
  John 48
  Luther 55, 61
  Nahum 48
  O. L. 27
  Richard 35

Spaulding, Solomon 24
Spencer, Elephas 37
  Elisha 37
  Israel 37
  Jonathan 37
  Phineas 37
Sperry, --- 66
Spooner, Ruggles 55
St. John, David B. 27
  Platt 50
Starkweather, George C. 52
Steere, Nicholas 34
  Rufus 34, 36
Sterriker, John W. 59
Stever, Henry 67
Stewart, Alvin 24
  James 26, 68
  William 68
Stickney, William 27
Stone, Benjamin 41
  Uriel 29
  William L. 52
Straight, Calvin 36
Strong, Chauncey 36
Sullivan, --- (Gen.) 6, 7, 44
Sutphen, John 59
  Peter 59
Swan, A. L. 9
Swart, Peter 44
Sweet, Jonathan 40
Swinyard, Thomas 19

# T

Talbot, George B. 27
  Jacob 27
Tanner, Ira 50
Taylor, --- (Elder) 27
  Erastus 49, 50
Teft, Jesse 50
Temple, Bernard 39
Thomas, Amos 29

Thomas, Hull 29
Thompson, James 24, 37
  John 37
  Nahum 26
Thorp, Edward 20
Thurber, Samuel 26
Thurston, Increase 5, 43
Treat, Charles 26
  John 26
Tripp, David 26
Tubbs, Seth 29
Tucker, Rufus 36
Tuckerman, George W. 9
Tuncliff, John 56
Tunnicliff, John 29
Turner, L. C. 13
Tyler, Eli 66
  Samuel 54
Tynart, Jacob 61

# U

Upton, Emory 10, 11, 13

# V

Van Schaick, Sybrant 4
VanWoert, Jacob 44

# W

Wadsworth, --- 10
Wainright, William P. 10
Wainwright, Charles S. 12
Wait, James 48
Waldo, Erastus 27
Wall, William R. 11
Walton, John 24
Warner, --- (Dr.) 68
Warren, --- (Gen.) 11
  Darius 49
Washbon, Ziba 41
Washington, --- (Gen.) 23
  George 49

Waterman, Elisha 26
  John 26, 67
  Lewis Edson 26
  Samuel 26, 66
Watson, Arnold B. 64
Wattles, Sluman 63
Weatherly, Daniel 36
Webster, Charles 66
Weed, Thurlow 52
Weller, Daniel 48
Wells, John 34
  Philip 34
Westcott, James 40
Wheeler, Henry 34
Whipple, Stephen 36
White, Green 67
  Joseph 24
Williams, Ashel 29
  Isaac 49
  Russell 50
  Samuel 55
Wilmot, William 63
Wilson, James 24

Wilson, John 24
Windsor, Amos 36
  Ezer 36
Winsor, Amos 34
  Joseph 34
Wolf, Conradt 44
  Jacob 44
Wright, Earl 37
  Elias 55
  Flavel 66
  Hiram 27
  John 66
  Martin 66

# Y

Yager, David 44
  Solomon 44
Yates, William 41
Young, --- 5
  Elias 11
  J. W. 9
  James 44, 61
  Robert 61

www.ingramcontent.com/pod-product-compliance
Lightning Source LLC
Chambersburg PA
CBHW051700090426
42736CB00013B/2471